Project 2010:
Basic
Student Manual

D1511597

Project 2010: Basic

Chief Executive Officer, Axzo Press:	Ken Wasnock
Series Designer and COO:	Adam A. Wilcox
Vice President, Operations:	Josh Pincus
Director of Publishing Systems Development:	Dan Quackenbush
Writer:	Brandon Heffernan
Copyeditor:	Catherine Oliver
Keytester:	Cliff Coryea

COPYRIGHT © 2010 Axzo Press. All rights reserved.

No part of this work may be reproduced, transcribed, or used in any form or by any means—graphic, electronic, or mechanical, including photocopying, recording, taping, Web distribution, or information storage and retrieval systems—without the prior written permission of the publisher.

For more information, go to www.logicaloperations.com

Trademarks

ILT Series is a trademark of Axzo Press.

Some of the product names and company names used in this book have been used for identification purposes only and may be trademarks or registered trademarks of their respective manufacturers and sellers.

Disclaimer

We reserve the right to revise this publication and make changes from time to time in its content without notice.

Student Manual

ISBN 10: 1-4260-2047-3
ISBN 13: 978-1-4260-2047-6

Printed in the United States of America

1 2 3 4 5 GL 06 05 04 03

Contents

Introduction   iii
    Topic A: About the manual.. iv
    Topic B: Setting your expectations..vii
    Topic C: Re-keying the course xii

Getting started   **1-1**
    Topic A: Project management concepts....................................1-2
    Topic B: The Project window 1-9
    Topic C: Project files 1-16
    Topic D: The Help window 1-19
    Unit summary: Getting started 1-21

Tasks   **2-1**
    Topic A: Creating a task list 2-2
    Topic B: Modifying a task list 2-9
    Topic C: The Work Breakdown Structure 2-13
    Unit summary: Tasks 2-21

Task scheduling   **3-1**
    Topic A: Task links..3-2
    Topic B: Task relationships 3-10
    Topic C: Task options...3-16
    Unit summary: Task scheduling...3-19

Resource management   **4-1**
    Topic A: The base calendar 4-2
    Topic B: Resources and calendars 4-6
    Topic C: Project costs...4-17
    Unit summary: Resource management..................................4-21

Views and tables   **5-1**
    Topic A: Working with views..5-2
    Topic B: Working with tables...5-10
    Unit summary: Views and tables...5-14

Filters, groups, and sorting   **6-1**
    Topic A: Filters...6-2
    Topic B: Groups 6-8
    Topic C: Sorting tasks and resources....................................6-12
    Unit summary: Filters, groups, and sorting 6-17

Finalizing the task plan   **7-1**
    Topic A: Finalizing schedules..7-2
    Topic B: Handling resource conflicts 7-8
    Unit summary: Finalizing the task plan 7-15

Course summary   S-1
Topic A: Course summary..S-2
Topic B: Continued learning after class.......................................S-4

Glossary   G-1

Index   I-1

Introduction

After reading this introduction, you will know how to:

A Use ILT Series manuals in general.

B Use prerequisites, a target student description, course objectives, and a skills inventory to properly set your expectations for the course.

C Re-key this course after class.

Topic A: About the manual

ILT Series philosophy

Our manuals facilitate your learning by providing structured interaction with the software itself. While we provide text to explain difficult concepts, the hands-on activities are the focus of our courses. By paying close attention as your instructor leads you through these activities, you will learn the skills and concepts effectively.

We believe strongly in the instructor-led class. During class, focus on your instructor. Our manuals are designed and written to facilitate your interaction with your instructor, and not to call attention to manuals themselves.

We believe in the basic approach of setting expectations, delivering instruction, and providing summary and review afterwards. For this reason, lessons begin with objectives and end with summaries. We also provide overall course objectives and a course summary to provide both an introduction to and closure on the entire course.

Manual components

The manuals contain these major components:

- Table of contents
- Introduction
- Units
- Appendix
- Course summary
- Glossary
- Index

Each element is described below.

Table of contents

The table of contents acts as a learning roadmap.

Introduction

The introduction contains information about our training philosophy and our manual components, features, and conventions. It contains target student, prerequisite, objective, and setup information for the specific course.

Units

Units are the largest structural component of the course content. A unit begins with a title page that lists objectives for each major subdivision, or topic, within the unit. Within each topic, conceptual and explanatory information alternates with hands-on activities. Units conclude with a summary comprising one paragraph for each topic, and an independent practice activity that gives you an opportunity to practice the skills you've learned.

The conceptual information takes the form of text paragraphs, exhibits, lists, and tables. The activities are structured in two columns, one telling you what to do, the other providing explanations, descriptions, and graphics.

Appendices

An appendix is similar to a unit in that it contains objectives and conceptual explanations. However, an appendix does not include hands-on activities, a summary, or an independent practice activity.

Course summary

This section provides a text summary of the entire course. It is useful for providing closure at the end of the course. The course summary also indicates the next course in this series, if there is one, and lists additional resources you might find useful as you continue to learn about the software.

Glossary

The glossary provides definitions for all of the key terms used in this course.

Index

The index at the end of this manual makes it easy for you to find information about a particular software component, feature, or concept.

Manual conventions

We've tried to keep the number of elements and the types of formatting to a minimum in the manuals. This aids in clarity and makes the manuals more classically elegant looking. But there are some conventions and icons you should know about.

Item	Description
Italic text	In conceptual text, indicates a new term or feature.
Bold text	In unit summaries, indicates a key term or concept. In an independent practice activity, indicates an explicit item that you select, choose, or type.
`Code font`	Indicates code or syntax.
`Longer strings of ▶ code will look ▶ like this.`	In the hands-on activities, any code that's too long to fit on a single line is divided into segments by one or more continuation characters (▶). This code should be entered as a continuous string of text.
Select **bold item**	In the left column of hands-on activities, bold sans-serif text indicates an explicit item that you select, choose, or type.
Keycaps like ⏎ ENTER	Indicate a key on the keyboard you must press.

Hands-on activities

The hands-on activities are the most important parts of our manuals. They are divided into two primary columns. The "Here's how" column gives short instructions to you about what to do. The "Here's why" column provides explanations, graphics, and clarifications. Here's a sample:

Do it!

A-1: Creating a commission formula

Here's how	Here's why
1 Open Sales	This is an oversimplified sales compensation worksheet. It shows sales totals, commissions, and incentives for five sales reps.
2 Observe the contents of cell F4	`F4  ▼   =  =E4*C_Rate` The commission rate formulas use the name "C_Rate" instead of a value for the commission rate.

For these activities, we have provided a collection of data files designed to help you learn each skill in a real-world business context. As you work through the activities, you will modify and update these files. Of course, you might make a mistake and therefore want to re-key the activity starting from scratch. To make it easy to start over, you will rename each data file at the end of the first activity in which the file is modified. Our convention for renaming files is to add the word "My" to the beginning of the file name. In the above activity, for example, a file called "Sales" is being used for the first time. At the end of this activity, you would save the file as "My sales," thus leaving the "Sales" file unchanged. If you make a mistake, you can start over using the original "Sales" file.

In some activities, however, it might not be practical to rename the data file. If you want to retry one of these activities, ask your instructor for a fresh copy of the original data file.

Topic B: Setting your expectations

Properly setting your expectations is essential to your success. This topic will help you do that by providing:

- Prerequisites for this course
- A description of the target student
- A list of the objectives for the course
- A skills assessment for the course

Course prerequisites

Before taking this course, you should be familiar with personal computers and the use of a keyboard and a mouse. Furthermore, this course assumes that you've completed the following course or have equivalent experience:

- *Windows XP: Basic*, *Windows Vista: Basic*, or *Windows 7: Basic*

Target student

Students taking this course should be comfortable using a personal computer and Microsoft Windows XP or later. You will get the most out of this course if your goal is to become a proficient project manager by using Microsoft Project 2010 to plan and manage your projects.

Course objectives

These overall course objectives will give you an idea about what to expect from the course. It is also possible that they will help you see that this course is not the right one for you. If you think you either lack the prerequisite knowledge or already know most of the subject matter to be covered, you should let your instructor know that you think you are misplaced in the class.

After completing this course, you will know how to:

- Discuss basic project management concepts and principles; identify project view options, interface components, and Gantt chart elements; create and save a project file; and get help on using Microsoft Project.

- Create a task list, using both manual and automatic scheduling modes; set durations; modify a task list; establish a Work Breakdown Structure; hide columns; set milestones; and format the Sheet pane and the Gantt chart.

- Link tasks to establish a project schedule; modify task predecessors; set lag time and lead time; add recurring tasks; work in Network Diagram view; modify task relationships; apply different task types; and set task constraints.

- Create a base calendar and edit the working time; create a resource pool and a resource calendar; assign resources to tasks; create and apply a task calendar; enter resource costs; and use the Cost table.

- Work in Calendar view and Resource Form view; add tasks to the Timeline; format the Timeline, and copy the Timeline to other Office applications; work with tables and create tables; and display WBS outline numbers.

- Apply filters, highlighting, AutoFilters, and custom filters; group tasks and resources; create custom groups; sort tasks and resources; and renumber a sorted task list or resource list.

- Display the critical path and slack; edit effort-driven schedules to fine-tune a project; and resolve resource conflicts by applying both automatic and manual resource leveling.

Skills inventory

Use the following form to gauge your skill level entering the class. For each skill listed, rate your familiarity from 1 to 5, with five being the most familiar. *This is not a test.* Rather, it is intended to provide you with an idea of where you're starting from at the beginning of class. If you're wholly unfamiliar with all the skills, you might not be ready for the class. If you think you already understand all of the skills, you might need to move on to the next course in the series. In either case, you should let your instructor know as soon as possible.

Skill	1	2	3	4	5
Identifying Project 2010 interface components					
Identifying Gantt chart elements					
Creating projects					
Switching between project views					
Setting the project start date					
Navigating Help topics					
Creating task lists					
Working in manual scheduling mode					
Working in automatic scheduling mode					
Changing the default scheduling mode					
Setting task durations					
Modifying task lists					
Rearranging tasks					
Formatting the Sheet pane					
Inserting project summary tasks					
Adding summary tasks and subtasks					
Hiding and showing subtasks					
Hiding columns in the Sheet pane					
Inserting milestone tasks					
Formatting a Gantt chart					
Linking and unlinking tasks					
Changing task predecessors					

Skill	1	2	3	4	5
Applying lead time and lag time					
Inserting recurring tasks					
Working in Network Diagram view					
Modifying task relationships					
Navigating a Gantt chart by using the Timeline					
Setting task types					
Setting task constraints					
Creating base calendars					
Changing the working time in a project calendar					
Creating resource pools					
Creating and applying resource calendars					
Assigning resources to tasks					
Creating and applying task calendars					
Entering project costs					
Using the Cost table					
Working with Calendar and form views					
Adding tasks to the Timeline					
Formatting the Timeline					
Copying the Timeline into other Office applications					
Displaying WBS outline numbers					
Creating and modifying tables					
Applying filters and AutoFilters					
Highlighting information					
Creating custom filters					
Grouping tasks and resources					
Creating custom groups					

Skill	1	2	3	4	5
Sorting tasks and resources					
Displaying critical tasks					
Displaying free slack					
Editing effort-driven schedules to fine-tune a project					
Applying automatic resource leveling					
Leveling resources manually					

Topic C: Re-keying the course

If you have the proper hardware and software, you can re-key this course after class. This section explains what you'll need in order to do so, and how to do it.

Hardware requirements

Your personal computer should have:

- A keyboard and a mouse
- A 1GHz (or faster) processor
- At least 1GB of RAM
- 2 GB of available hard disk space after operating system install
- A CD-ROM or DVD drive
- A monitor at 1024 × 768 or higher resolution

Software requirements

You will also need the following software:

- Windows 7, Windows Vista, or Windows XP with Service Pack 3
- Project Standard 2010 or Project Professional 2010
- PowerPoint 2010 (This is required to complete Activity A-4 in Unit 5, "Views and tables," but is not used elsewhere in the course.)

Network requirements

The following network components and connectivity are also required for re-keying this course:

- Internet access, for the following purposes:
    - Downloading the latest critical updates and service packs

Setup instructions to re-key the course

Before you re-key the course, you will need to perform the following steps.

1   Use Windows Update to install all available critical updates and Service Packs.

2   With flat-panel displays, we recommend using the panel's native resolution for best results. Color depth/quality should be set to High (24 bit) or higher.

Please note that your display settings or resolution may differ from the author's, so your screens might not exactly match the screen shots in this manual.

3   If necessary, reset any defaults that you have changed. If you do not wish to reset the defaults, you can still re-key the course, but some activities might not work exactly as documented.

4   If you have the data disc that came with this manual, locate the Student Data folder on it and copy it to the desktop of your computer.

If you don't have the data disc, you can download the Student Data files for the course:

a   Connect to http://downloads.logicaloperations.com.

b   Enter the course title or search by part to locate this course

c   Click the course title to display a list of available downloads.
    Note: Data Files are located under the Instructor Edition of the course.

d   Click the link(s) for downloading the Student Data files.

e   Create a folder named Student Data on the desktop of your computer.

f   Double-click the downloaded zip file(s) and drag the contents into the Student Data folder.

Unit 1
Getting started

Unit time: 50 minutes

Complete this unit, and you'll know how to:

A Discuss basic project management concepts and principles, and identify project view options.

B Start Project, open a project file, and identify interface components and Gantt chart elements.

C Create and save a project file.

D Get help with using Microsoft Project.

Topic A: Project management concepts

Explanation

As a project manager, you have to manage and control your project to make it a success. You'll need to understand project management concepts and apply them. You can use Microsoft Project 2010 to help you to organize, track, and manage your project effectively.

Keys to successful project management

A *project* is a series of steps that are performed to reach a specific goal. Projects have a definite start and end, and they result in a product or service. Projects are often the critical components of the performing organization's business strategy. A project has three general constraints:

- **Scope** — Customer requirements, quality specifications, and deliverables
- **Cost** — Budget and resources
- **Time** — Timelines for tasks and specific start and end dates

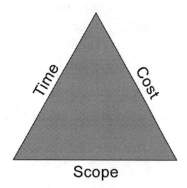

Exhibit 1-1: The constraints of a project

A project is considered successful when it's delivered on time, stays within budget, and meets customer requirements. To manage your project effectively, it can be helpful to break it into phases so that it's easier to control. The five phases of a project are:

- The initial phase
- The planning phase
- The implementation phase
- The monitoring phase
- The close-out phase

Collectively, these phases make up the project life cycle. Each phase is marked by the completion of one or more deliverables, called *milestones*.

Project management

Project management is the application of knowledge, skills, tools, and techniques to accomplish activities or tasks to meet the objectives set for a project. To manage a project, you need to understand the phases involved in project management; these phases are the defining of priorities, limitations, and constraints for the project. They describe and organize the work of the project. Exhibit 1-2 illustrates the links between the phases in a project's life cycle.

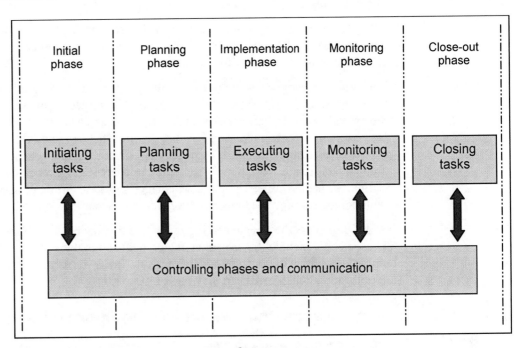

Exhibit 1-2: The links between project phases

The project management phases are described in the following table.

Phase	Description
Initial	Establish the beginning of the project and define the project's objectives and scope.
Planning	Devise and maintain a workable scheme to meet the objectives and business needs of the project. Also, identify the tasks and their resource requirements.
Implementation	Execute tasks and coordinate people and other resources to carry out the plan.
Monitoring	Track and report on the project's progress. *Monitoring* involves reviewing the progress of the project, compared to the plan, and leads to control measures being taken. *Control* means taking corrective measures to ensure the success of the project.
Close-out	Formalize the acceptance of the project, ensure an orderly end, and evaluate personnel and the project itself for lessons learned.

Constraints

As you track and control the project to ensure that it progresses smoothly, you need to consider the constraints that the project might face. *Constraints* are the limitations imposed on a project. You can manage constraints by minimizing risks, costs, and resources. However, *time* is the main constraint that affects the performance of a project. You can manage your project effectively if you allocate proper time frames for each project phase.

Project roles

Projects often require a team of people with different roles and responsibilities to communicate with each other and work together. The cohesiveness of this group can affect the project's successful completion.

The *project manager* has the primary role of directing the project's flow and the communication between project participants. The project manager leads the planning of the project, watches for cost overruns, and manages disputes. He or she is responsible for *risk management,* preparing for uncertainties that can and often will occur during a project. This person must also manage scope changes to prevent *scope creep,* the gradual addition of work which eventually makes the original cost and schedule estimates unachievable. The project manager's process for dealing with scope changes will include revising the budget and schedule to accommodate project changes.

Stakeholders are the people and organizations that have a vested interest in the project. These people include the project manager, decision makers, customers, vendors, and employees who will contribute to the project. These roles can be filled by one or more people, and an individual can play one or more roles.

Do it!

A-1: Discussing project management concepts

Questions and answers
1 What is a project?
2 Why is planning necessary for a project?
3 Why must you always monitor your project?
4 What is project management?
5 Which project management phase involves the execution of tasks and the coordination of people and other resources to carry out the plan?
6 What are the primary responsibilities of the project manager?
7 What are constraints?
8 What is scope creep?

Introduction to Microsoft Project 2010

Explanation

Managing a project can become difficult if it's not planned well. A project can fail if the time required to complete it exceeds the planned duration, if the total cost exceeds the planned budget, or if the end deliverable or product does not meet planned expectations. By using Microsoft Project, you can more effectively organize, schedule, and manage your project.

Project management tasks

There are several things you'll need to do to manage your project effectively and meet your project's objectives. Exhibit 1-3 shows a sample breakdown of typical project management tasks.

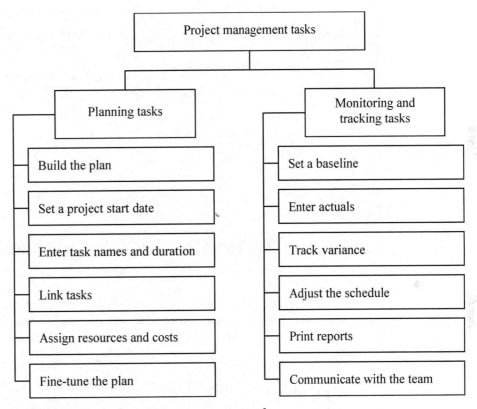

Exhibit 1-3: Typical project management tasks

Resources

Resources are the people, materials, and equipment that enable you to complete project tasks. Microsoft Project helps you keep track of the resources assigned to accomplish each task.

Overview of Project 2010 views

You can use a variety of views to focus on specific aspects of your project. These include Gantt Chart view, Network Diagram view, Calendar view, Resource Sheet view, and Resource Usage view. In all views, the Timeline is displayed by default. It appears just below the Ribbon. If you prefer not to use the Timeline, click the View tab and clear the Timeline box.

Gantt Chart view

Gantt Chart view is Project's default view. It's separated into two panes—with the Sheet pane on the left, and the Chart pane on the right—as shown in Exhibit 1-4. The Timeline is displayed across the top of the two panes.

You use Gantt Chart view to enter and view task-related information. The Sheet pane shows your task list. The Chart pane displays tasks and task relationships graphically.

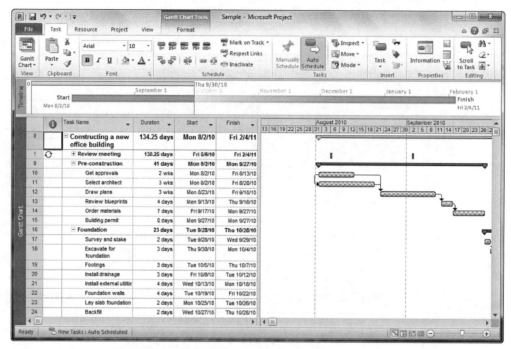

Exhibit 1-4: Gantt Chart view, with the Timeline active

You will likely spend much of your time working in Gantt Chart view, and one of the first things you'll need to do is establish your task list, also known as the *Work Breakdown Structure (WBS)*. The WBS is a hierarchical arrangement of tasks, as shown in Exhibit 1-5.

		Task Name	Duration	Start	Finish
0		⊟ **Constructing a new office building**	**134.25 days**	**Mon 8/2/10**	**Fri 2/4/11**
1	⟳	⊞ **Review meeting**	130.25 days	Fri 8/6/10	Fri 2/4/11
9		⊟ **Pre-construction**	41 days	Mon 8/2/10	Mon 9/27/10
10		Get approvals	2 wks	Mon 8/2/10	Fri 8/13/10
11		Select architect	3 wks	Mon 8/2/10	Fri 8/20/10
12		Draw plans	3 wks	Mon 8/23/10	Fri 9/10/10
13		Review blueprints	4 days	Mon 9/13/10	Thu 9/16/10
14		Order materials	7 days	Fri 9/17/10	Mon 9/27/10
15		Building permit	0 days	Mon 9/27/10	Mon 9/27/10

Exhibit 1-5: A task list in Gantt Chart view

Network Diagram view

Network Diagram view displays project details as a flowchart that shows how tasks are arranged. This view can help you visualize and analyze task relationships.

Calendar view

You can use Calendar view to display your project dates chronologically or to evaluate effort (the amount of work assigned in a given time period) in calendar days.

Resource Sheet view

Project also provides various views for working with resource assignments and costs. You can enter resource information in Resource Sheet view, shown in Exhibit 1-6.

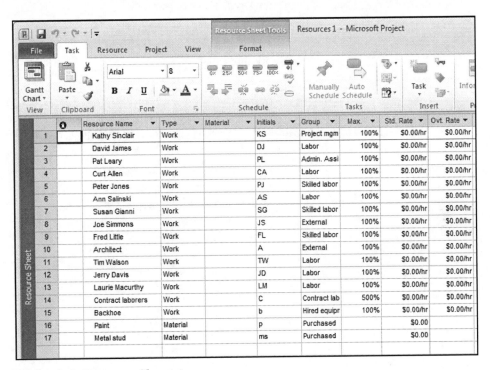

	Resource Name	Type	Material	Initials	Group	Max.	Std. Rate	Ovt. Rate
1	Kathy Sinclair	Work		KS	Project mgm	100%	$0.00/hr	$0.00/hr
2	David James	Work		DJ	Labor	100%	$0.00/hr	$0.00/hr
3	Pat Leary	Work		PL	Admin. Assi	100%	$0.00/hr	$0.00/hr
4	Curt Allen	Work		CA	Labor	100%	$0.00/hr	$0.00/hr
5	Peter Jones	Work		PJ	Skilled labor	100%	$0.00/hr	$0.00/hr
6	Ann Salinski	Work		AS	Labor	100%	$0.00/hr	$0.00/hr
7	Susan Gianni	Work		SG	Skilled labor	100%	$0.00/hr	$0.00/hr
8	Joe Simmons	Work		JS	External	100%	$0.00/hr	$0.00/hr
9	Fred Little	Work		FL	Skilled labor	100%	$0.00/hr	$0.00/hr
10	Architect	Work		A	External	100%	$0.00/hr	$0.00/hr
11	Tim Walson	Work		TW	Labor	100%	$0.00/hr	$0.00/hr
12	Jerry Davis	Work		JD	Labor	100%	$0.00/hr	$0.00/hr
13	Laurie Macurthy	Work		LM	Labor	100%	$0.00/hr	$0.00/hr
14	Contract laborers	Work		C	Contract lab	500%	$0.00/hr	$0.00/hr
15	Backhoe	Work		b	Hired equipr	100%	$0.00/hr	$0.00/hr
16	Paint	Material		p	Purchased		$0.00	
17	Metal stud	Material		ms	Purchased		$0.00	

Exhibit 1-6: Resource Sheet view

Resource Usage view

After entering resource information, you can switch to Resource Usage view to monitor the number of hours each resource is scheduled for, and the tasks to which they are assigned.

Do it! **A-2: Discussing project management tools**

Questions and answers
1 What is a Gantt chart?
2 What is the Work Breakdown Structure?
3 What is a network diagram?
4 How can Calendar view help you manage a project?
5 What are some typical project management tasks?

Topic B: The Project window

Explanation

After you plan the basic tasks needed to accomplish your project, you can start working with Microsoft Project 2010. When you start Project, a new project file called Project1 is displayed in Gantt Chart view in the Project window. You can begin entering task details, or create a new project based on one of many templates available at Office.com.

Microsoft Project 2010 interface components

Exhibit 1-7 shows the main interface components of Microsoft Project 2010.

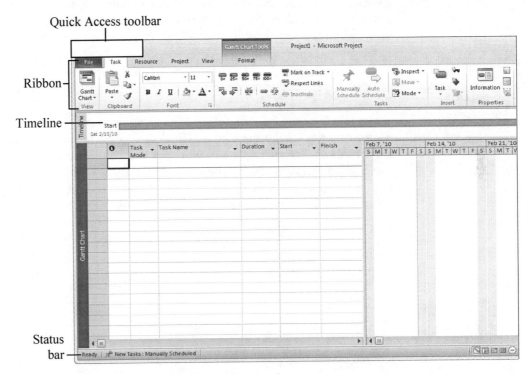

Exhibit 1-7: The Microsoft Project 2010 interface

The following table describes the Project 2010 interface components.

Component	Description
Quick Access toolbar	Displays commands for saving the current project, undoing the last action, and repeating the last action. You can personalize the Quick Access toolbar by adding buttons for commands you use frequently. You can also move the Quick Access toolbar below the Ribbon.
Ribbon	The main location for menus and commands. The Ribbon has several tabs that contain groups of related commands.
Timeline	Provides a "big picture" view of your project. You can copy your project Timeline and share it with other Office applications. By default, Gantt Chart view is active with the Timeline at the top. You can switch to Timeline view to maximize the display of the Timeline.
Status bar	Displays the current status of the project file, and information about a selected command or an operation in progress.

The Ribbon interface

The Ribbon interface was introduced in Office 2007 applications and is new to Project 2010. The Ribbon is the main location for menus and tools. When you click a Ribbon tab (such as Task, Resource, or Project), it displays various groups of related tools. Some tools are buttons you click to take an immediate action, and other tools display menus, lists, or galleries with more options. (A *gallery* is a collection of style options that are represented graphically to provide a preview.)

Some of the commands and options that are available on the Ribbon are contextual, meaning that they change based on the current view. For example, when you're working in Gantt Chart view, the Ribbon displays the Gantt Chart Tools | Format tab. If you switch to Resource Sheet view, the Ribbon will display the Resource Sheet Tools | Format tab. The commands and options on the Format tab change the most from view to view, while the other tabs show dimmed (unavailable) commands if they cannot be used in the current view.

Backstage view

When you click the File tab, "Backstage view" is displayed. This feature is new to all Microsoft Office 2010 applications. Backstage view provides a central location for commands used to take action on a project as a whole, such as creating a file, saving a file, and preparing to print. Exhibit 1-8 shows Backstage view with the New command selected. From here, you can create a new blank project, start a new project file based on another file, or use free templates available at Office.com.

Exhibit 1-8: The File tab displays Backstage view

Do it!

B-1: Identifying interface components

Here's how	Here's why
1 Click **Start** and choose **All Programs**, **Microsoft Office**, **Microsoft Project 2010**	To start Microsoft Project 2010.
In the Welcome to Microsoft Office 2010 screen, select **Don't make changes** and click **OK**	If necessary.
2 Observe the title bar	It shows that a new blank file, with the default name Project1, is open. The Gantt Chart tools are displayed by default.
3 Locate the Quick Access toolbar	(In the top-left corner of the window.) It contains commands for saving the current project, undoing the last action, and repeating the last action. You can personalize the Quick Access toolbar by adding buttons for commands you use frequently.
4 Observe the Ribbon tabs	The Task tab is active by default. There are also File, Resource, Project, View, and Format tabs.
5 Observe the Task tab	Commands on the Ribbon are grouped logically. The Task tab contains the View group of commands, along with the Clipboard, Font, Schedule, Tasks, Insert, and Properties groups.
6 In the Properties group, point to Information	A ScreenTip appears. You can point to commands on the Ribbon to read brief command descriptions and to see keyboard shortcuts when available.
7 Click the **Resource** tab	To display resource-related commands.
8 Click the **Project** tab	On this tab, you can modify project information, change the working time, move the project calendar, and generate reports, among other things.
9 Double-click the **Project** tab	To hide the Ribbon and get more screen space in which to work. The tabs remain visible so that you can easily activate the Ribbon again.
10 Double-click the **Task** tab	To activate the Ribbon with the Task tab active.
11 Locate the Timeline	By default, the Timeline is displayed at the top of Gantt Chart view. It provides a "big-picture" view of your project.

12 Locate the status bar	The status bar shows the current state of the Project window, and provides tools for switching the view of the current Project file and for zooming in and out on the current file.
13 Click the **File** tab	To display Backstage view, which provides options for taking action on Project files, such as opening and closing files, saving files, and setting print options.
14 Click **Close**	
Click **No**	(If necessary.) To close the blank file without saving it. The application remains open. The commands are inactive because there's no Project file open.

Gantt Chart elements

Explanation

Gantt Chart view is divided into two panes, as shown in Exhibit 1-9. The Sheet pane, on the left, resembles a spreadsheet, with rows, columns, and cells. You insert task names in the cells under the column headings. Each column displays information that is stored in the Project file. The row numbers are the IDs for the tasks.

The Chart pane, on the right, displays the information in the Sheet pane graphically. A bar represents a task, and the length of a bar shows the duration of that task. You can easily compare the start and finish dates of tasks by comparing the length of their task bars. Gantt Chart view also displays a default timescale, which shows the month and days on a weekly basis.

You can use the horizontal and vertical scroll bars in each pane to display the columns that are outside the current viewing area.

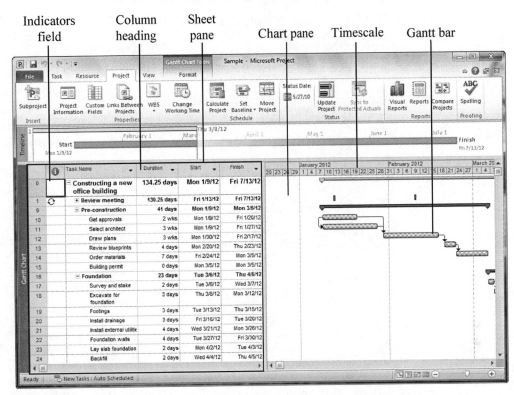

Exhibit 1-9: A project file in Gantt Chart view, with the Project tab active

The following table describes the components of Gantt Chart view.

Component	Description
Indicators field	Displays icons that represent information about a task. There are indicators for many things, including constraints, notes, and over-allocated resources.
Column heading	Displays the field name in the Sheet pane.
Sheet pane	A spreadsheet, consisting of rows, columns, and cells that contain project data.
Chart pane	Displays task information as graphical bars corresponding to task duration.
Timescale	Indicates the timeframe shown in the Gantt chart.
Gantt bar	(Also called a *task bar*.) Represents a task. The longer the Gantt bar, the longer the duration of the task.

To open a Project file and start working with it:

1 Click the File tab and then click Open. The Open dialog box appears.

2 Navigate to the Project file that you want to open and select it.

3 Click Open (or double-click the file).

Do it!

B-2: Exploring Gantt Chart view

The files for this activity are in Student Data folder **Unit 1\Topic B**.

Here's how	Here's why
1 Click the **File** tab	
Click **Open**	The Open dialog box appears.
2 Open the **Student Data** folder	On the Windows desktop.
Open the current unit folder	
Open the current topic folder	
3 Select **Sample** and click **Open**	You'll use this Project file to explore different views. The project opens in Gantt Chart view, which consists of the Sheet pane and the Chart pane. The Timeline at the top spans both panes.
4 Observe the Sheet pane	The Sheet pane displays the project's task list. Each row represents a task, and each row number represents a task ID.
Observe the column headings	Each view has different default columns. Each column displays information from the Project file. The default columns in Gantt Chart view include Task Name, Duration, Start, and Finish.
At the bottom of the Sheet pane, scroll horizontally	To view the other default column headings.
Scroll back to the left	If necessary.
5 Observe the Indicators column	(The leftmost column in the Sheet pane.) This column displays icons that indicate task-related information.
Point to the circling arrow icon	(In the Indicators column.) A ScreenTip appears, indicating that the task in this row repeats seven times. There are several other icons that appear when certain conditions apply.

6 Point to the divider bar, as shown

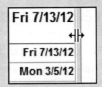

The pointer changes to a double-headed arrow when placed on the divider bar. You can drag it either way to change the width of a pane.

Drag to the left

To increase the width of the Chart pane and decrease the width of the Sheet pane.

7 Observe the Chart pane

The Chart pane displays the information in the Sheet pane in a graphical format.

8 Observe the timescale

(In the Chart pane.) It shows the months and days of the week.

9 Observe the task bars

The length of a task bar depicts the duration of that task. Using the timescale, you can quickly see the start and end dates for each task.

Point to any task bar

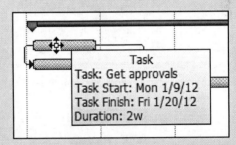

(Any one of the blue bars in the chart.) Details about the task are displayed.

Click a task bar

Its corresponding task is selected in the Sheet pane.

10 Click the gray bar at the top of the chart, as shown

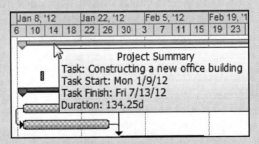

This is the project summary task. It represents a summary of all project tasks and the project timeline from start to finish.

11 Click the **File** tab

Click **Close**

Click **No**

Topic C: Project files

Explanation

When you start Microsoft Project, a new project file appears in Gantt Chart view by default. You can start working with this default project file, or you can create a new project file, create a project file based on a template, or open an existing project file.

The Project Information dialog box

When you create a project file, you're not prompted to supply any project information. A good place to get started is the Project Information dialog box. To open it, click the Project tab. Then, in the Properties group, click Project Information.

By default, the Project Information dialog box uses the current date as the project start date. (The finish date is calculated by Project after all of your task information is established and linked.) To set a different start date, click the arrow in the Start date field and select a date from the calendar.

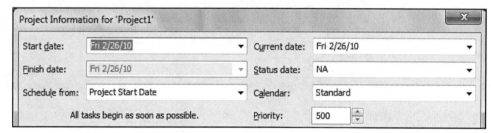

Exhibit 1-10: The Project Information dialog box

Defining project properties

In the Project Properties dialog box, you can enter general project information, such as the project name, the project manager's name, the name of your organization, and specific keywords related to the project. This information will help you organize and locate your project files.

To define properties for your project, open the project, click the File tab, and click Info. In the right pane, click Project Information and choose Advanced Properties. This opens the Project Properties dialog box. Enter values on the Summary tab, and click OK.

Do it!

C-1:   Creating a project file

Here's how	Here's why
1 Click the **File** tab	The New command is selected on the File tab, and "Blank project" is selected by default under "Available Templates."
In the right pane, click **Create**	
2 Click the **Project** tab	
In the Properties group, click **Project Information**	To open the Project Information dialog box. By default, the current date is set as the project start date. The finish date is calculated by Project after you enter your task information.
3 In the Start date field, click the arrow	A calendar appears.
Select a date that is one month from today's date	
Click **OK**	To close the Project Information dialog box.
4 Click the **File** tab	
Click **Info**	If necessary.
5 In the right pane, click **Project Information**	
Choose **Advanced Properties**	The Properties dialog box opens with the Summary tab active. You'll enter information in the various fields.
6 In the Title box, type **Construct a new office building**	
Edit the other fields to read as shown	Author: David James Manager: David James Company: Outlander Spices
Click **OK**	To close the dialog box.

Saving project files

Explanation

After you have created a project file and specified a start date for your project, you need to save the file to preserve the information for future use. The first time you save a project file, you specify its file name and storage location. Later, as you're working on the project, you can click Save or press Ctrl+S to quickly update the file, using the same name and location.

To save a project file for the first time:

1 On the Quick Access toolbar, click the Save button (or press Ctrl+S).
2 In the Save As dialog box, navigate to the location where you want to save the project file (or accept the default location).
3 In the File name box, type a name for the project file.
4 Click Save (or press Enter).

Do it!

C-2: Saving a project file

Here's how	Here's why
1 On the Quick Access toolbar, click 🖫	The Save As dialog box opens because this is the first time this file has been saved.
2 In the navigation pane, under Favorites, click **Desktop**	
Double-click the **Student Data** folder	Scroll down, if necessary.
Open the current unit folder	
Open the current topic folder	You'll save the project file in this folder.
3 Edit the File name box to read **My new project**	
4 Click **Save**	To save the file in the specified folder.
5 Observe the title bar	The title bar updates to show the name of the project file.
6 Click the **File** tab	
Click **Close**	

Topic D: The Help window

Explanation

You can use Project's Help window to get assistance while you're working. To open the Project Help window, click the Help button or press F1.

If your computer is connected to the Internet, the Help window displays live content from Office.com. If you're offline, the Help window displays content that was installed along with the program on your computer. You don't need to open a project file to open the Project Help window.

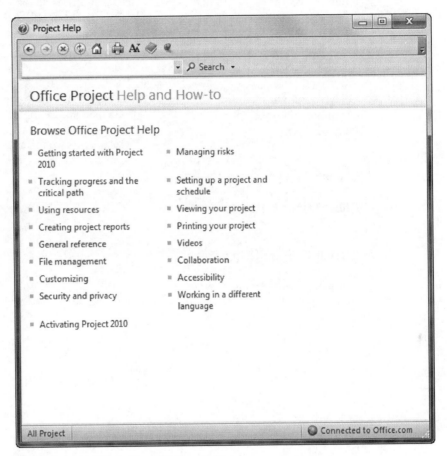

Exhibit 1-11: The Project Help window

Do it!

D-1: Getting help with using Project

Here's how	Here's why
1 On the right side of the program window, click 🔵	To open the Project Help window. If your computer is connected to the Internet, the Help window displays live content from Office.com. If you're working offline, local Help content is displayed.
2 Click the first item in the list	To display that Help topic. This content is downloaded from Office.com.
3 Click the arrow to the right of the Search button	
Under "Content from this computer," choose **Project Help**	To access local Help content, which was installed on your computer with the program. Your computer doesn't have to be connected to the Internet for you to access this Help content.
4 In the Search box, enter **saving**	
Click **Save as PDF or XPS**	To view information on how to save a project file in PDF or XPS format.
5 Close the Project Help window	
6 Close Microsoft Project	

Unit summary: Getting started

Topic A
In this topic, you learned basic **project management concepts**. You learned about the phases of a project and the many ways that Project 2010 can help you manage projects successfully. You also learned about the various **project views** you can use as you manage your projects.

Topic B
In this topic, you learned how to create a project and open a project file. You identified Project's **interface components** and the elements of a **Gantt chart**.

Topic C
In this topic, you learned how to create a project file and use the Project Information dialog box to set the **start date** for a project. You also learned how to use the **Properties** dialog box to enter general project information, and you learned how to save a new project file.

Topic D
In this topic, you learned how to use the Project **Help** window, and you learned how to search for Help topics when you're offline.

Independent practice activity

In this activity, you'll create and save a project file. You'll also set a project start date, set project properties, and use the Project Help window.

1 Start Microsoft Project 2010.

2 Create a project file.

3 Set the start date as two months from today.

4 Save the project as **My practice project** in the current Unit summary folder.

5 Specify the properties shown in Exhibit 1-12. (*Hint:* Click the File tab and then click Info.)

6 Open the Project Help window and enter **timescale** in the Search box.

7 Click the first topic in the list of results.

8 Close the Project Help window.

9 Save and close the project file.

10 Close Microsoft Project.

Exhibit 1-12: The Project Properties dialog box

Review questions

1 What are the five project management phases?

2 During the _____ phase, you devise a workable scheme to meet project objectives and identify the tasks and their resource requirements.

3 How do you set the project start date?

4 What are some other project views that are available?

5 How can you get help as you work in Project?

6 What is a Gantt bar?

7 The _____ indicates the timeframe shown in the Gantt chart.

Unit 2
Tasks

Unit time: 75 minutes

Complete this unit, and you'll know how to:

A Create a task list by using both manual and automatic scheduling modes, change the task scheduling mode, and set durations.

B Modify a task list and format text in the Sheet pane.

C Establish a Work Breakdown Structure, hide columns, set milestones, and apply Gantt Chart styles.

Topic A: Creating a task list

Explanation

Every activity in a project is a *task*. There are many ways to get started with a task list, depending on the nature of the project and your own project management style. You can begin your project planning by listing the major phases as summary tasks and then identifying the subtasks for each of those phases. As you identify the tasks for your project, you can estimate the time needed to accomplish each task.

The task list

The *task list* is a complete list of project tasks and subtasks. To create a task list, you enter all of the tasks that must be accomplished to complete the project. This list helps you decide what resources and time you'll need to complete the project. For example, if your project is to build a new office building, one major phase is to lay the foundation. Subtasks that would fall under the broad task of "Foundation" might include "survey and stake," "excavation," "footings," "drainage," and so on.

You enter task information as rows in the Sheet pane of Gantt Chart view and list them in their order of occurrence.

User-controlled scheduling

Project 2010 introduces a new feature called *user-controlled scheduling*. In previous versions of Project, the built-in scheduling engine was always on. In Project 2010, the default task scheduling mode is manual, meaning that Project will not automatically calculate the schedule as you enter tasks and task relationships. This way, if you're just getting started on a project but you don't have any details just yet, you can plug in some general information in lieu of those details. Then, as you get further into the project and more details emerge, you can switch to automatic scheduling to take advantage of Project's scheduling engine.

Manual scheduling mode

In manual scheduling mode, you determine the start date and duration of each task, and Project does not alter that task schedule. No default values are applied when you enter tasks, because at the outset of a typical project you might not have exact dates or a precise understanding of task durations.

Depending on the nature of your project, you might want to control how each task is scheduled. You can use the Task Mode column to indicate whether a task is manually or automatically scheduled. For example, you can manually schedule specific tasks while using automatic scheduling for all other tasks, or you can change the task mode for all tasks. You might want to use manual scheduling during the planning or proposal phase of a project, entering estimates to provide a general idea of the project schedule, and then switch to automatic scheduling once the project is approved and tasks are better defined.

Copying information between Project and other applications

You can paste content from other Office applications directly into your Project 2010 file. This can save you time entering general task information. For example, if your manager or colleague sends you an Outlook e-mail message with a bulleted list of initial tasks to consider for the project, you can copy the list, paste it directly into the Sheet pane, and then add further details as needed.

You can also share project information with stakeholders by pasting content from your Project file into other Office applications. For example, if you're in the initial stages of your project planning and you want to share your preliminary task list, you can copy it and paste it into an Outlook e-mail message, and it will retain all formatting.

Do it!

A-1:   Exploring user-controlled scheduling

Here's how	Here's why
1 Start Microsoft Project 2010	A new blank project file opens by default. You'll enter preliminary information about the project.
2 Click under Task Name	
Type **New office building**	
Press (↵ ENTER)	The task is entered with an ID of 1. Project does not enter any default duration or schedule value.
3 Type **Plan and design**	
Press (↵ ENTER)	Notice that without a duration value, nothing is displayed in the Chart pane.
4 Enter a task named **Foundation**	
5 In the Duration field for task 1, enter **10 months**	To enter an approximate duration value.
Observe the Duration value	It is automatically abbreviated as "10 mons."
Observe the task bar	A faded blue bar indicates that no start or finish date is set.
6 Click in the Start field for task 1	An arrow appears in the cell.
Click the arrow and click **Today**	To enter today's date as the project start date. You can always move the project later.
Observe the task bar	Now that the task has a start date, the task bar does not look faded.
7 In the Duration field for task 2, enter **5**	The default unit of time is days; Project automatically adds "days" to the numeric value.
Set the start date to a few days from today	
8 In the Duration field for task 3, enter **Ask Kathy**	Manual scheduling mode allows you to enter informal values such as this, which you can replace when project details are clarified.

9 Point to the first task bar, as shown

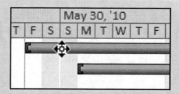

The pointer changes to indicate that you can move the task bar.

Drag to the right to move the task bar a few days forward

Observe the value in the Start field

The value in the field has been updated.

10 Drag the bar for task 2 to a few days after the task 1 start date

11 How might you take advantage of the user-controlled scheduling feature?

12 Save the project file as **My project start**

In the current topic folder.

Close the project file

Automatic scheduling

To take advantage of Project's scheduling engine, you need to work in automatic scheduling mode. If you're working with a project file built in manual scheduling mode, you can switch to automatic scheduling by clicking the Task Mode column header to select all tasks and then clicking Auto Schedule on the Task tab. You can convert individual tasks to automatic scheduling by clicking in the Task Mode field for a task and selecting Auto Scheduled. If you make a task auto-scheduled, Project determines its schedule based on factors such as constraints and dependencies.

If you're just getting started and you prefer to use Project's scheduling engine, you can set all new tasks to use automatic scheduling. In the status bar, click "New Tasks: Manually Scheduled" and select Auto Scheduled. This changes the scheduling mode only for new tasks entered in the current project file, and does not affect other project files.

Task durations

After you identify and list your tasks, you need to plan the duration of each task. You specify the duration of a task by entering a value in the Duration column. The default time period is days—if you enter a numeric value in a Duration field, "days" is automatically appended to the value. To specify a task duration in hours, you can enter a value followed by "h," as in 8h. To specify a value in weeks, you can type a value followed by "w," as in 2w.

A question mark after a duration value indicates an automatic estimate. You can change estimated durations to actual ones as needed or when more details emerge. When a Duration field is selected, it changes to a spinner box. Click the up arrow to increase a duration value, and click the down arrow to decrease it.

The task bars (the horizontal blue bars) in the Chart pane graphically represent the durations of the tasks. These bars look a bit different in automatic scheduling mode than they do in manual scheduling mode.

Do it! ## A-2: Adding tasks and durations in auto schedule mode

The files for this activity are in Student Data folder **Unit 2\Topic A**.

Here's how	Here's why
1 Create a new blank project file	(Click the File tab, click New, and then click Create.) You'll change the scheduling mode, create a task list, and set the duration of each task.
2 Click the **Project** tab	
Click **Project Information**	(In the Properties group.) To open the Project Information dialog box.
In the Start date box, enter a date two months from today	To set the start date for the project.
Click **OK**	To close the dialog box.
3 In the status bar, click as shown	
Select **Auto Scheduled**	So that your task dates will be calculated and updated automatically. Changing this setting affects only the current project file.
4 Click the first cell in the Task Name column	To select it. You'll enter the first task.
Type **Select architect**	
5 Press (TAB)	To move to the Duration field.
Observe the selected cell	"1 day?" appears by default. A question mark after a duration value indicates an estimated duration. In the Chart pane, the default length of the blue task bar also corresponds to one day.
6 In the Duration field, type **3w**	Project recognizes the "w" as an abbreviation for "weeks."
Press (↵ ENTER)	
Observe the task duration	The duration value does not have a question mark after it because it's no longer an estimated duration. The length of the task bar increases accordingly. Also, the "w" changes to "wks."

7 In the Task Name column, select
  the second cell

  Type **Get approvals**

  Press (TAB)   To move to the Duration field for this task.

8 In the Duration field, enter **2w**   To set the task's duration in weeks.

9 Observe the Chart pane

The second task bar is shorter than the first,
indicating that the second task has a shorter
duration than the first task.

10 Enter the new task details shown

Draw plans	3 wks
Review blueprints	4 days

11 Save the project file as   In the current topic folder.
   Construction project

   Close the file   Click the File tab and then click Close.

Changing the default scheduling mode for all new files

Explanation

You've already learned how to change the default scheduling mode for all new tasks within a particular project file. However, if you prefer to work with Project's scheduling engine at all times, you can change Project's default setting so that all new files use automatic scheduling. Here's how:

1 Click the File tab.

2 Click Options to open the Project Options dialog box.

3 Click Schedule.

4 From the "Scheduling options for this project" list, select All New Projects. (If no project file is open, this option will be selected automatically.)

5 From the "New tasks created" list, select Auto Scheduled.

6 Click OK.

Do it!

A-3: Changing the scheduling mode for all new files

Here's how	Here's why
1 Click the **File** tab	
2 Click **Options**	(Near the bottom of the left pane.) To open the Project Options dialog box.
Click **Schedule**	To display the schedule options.
3 In the "Scheduling options for this project" list, verify that **All New Projects** is selected	If a project file were open, you would need to select this option from the list.
4 From the "New tasks created" list, select **Auto Scheduled**	All future project files will use automatic scheduling.
Click **OK**	

Topic B: Modifying a task list

Explanation
You've already learned how to build a task structure by entering a series of tasks in the Task Name column. You can also insert new tasks between existing tasks. During the project life cycle, you will likely need to add or delete planned tasks, and move tasks to rearrange them in the project.

Adding tasks to a task list

To add tasks to a task list:

1   In the Task Name column, select the cell below the location where you want to insert the new task.

2   On the Task tab, in the Insert group, click the Insert Task button.

3   Type the task information in the new row.

You can also right-click the cell below the location where you want to insert the new task and choose Insert Task, or select the cell below the desired location and press Insert.

Deleting tasks

In the course of a typical project, you might need to delete tasks that are no longer necessary. To delete a task from the task list, do either of the following:

- Right-click the task and choose Delete Task.
- Select a row and press Delete.

B-1:   Inserting and deleting tasks

The files for this activity are in Student Data folder **Unit 2\Topic B**.

Here's how	Here's why
1 Open Construction	(From the current topic folder.) This project file contains a list of tasks. You'll insert and delete tasks.
Save the project file as **My Construction**	Click the File tab, click Save As, edit the file name, and click Save.
2 Select a cell in row 1	(Any cell will do.) You'll insert a task above this row.
3 On the Task tab, click as shown	To insert a new task.
4 Type **Pre-construction**	
Press (↵ ENTER)	
5 Right-click **Foundation walls**	(Task 15.) You'll add a task above this task.
Choose **Insert Task**	
Type **Prepare foundation** and press (↵ ENTER)	
6 Select **Level the ground**	(Task 9.) You'll delete this task.
Press (DELETE)	To clear the data. The cell remains selected, and a Delete icon appears to the left of it.
7 Click ☒	Two options are displayed. By default, only the contents of the cell are cleared.
Select **Delete the entire task**	The task is deleted and the task list is renumbered automatically.
8 Click **15**	(The row number.) To select the row for task 15.
Press (DELETE)	To delete the task. With this method, the entire task is deleted automatically.
9 Save your changes	Click the Save button or press Ctrl+S.

Rearranging tasks

Explanation

While examining the task list, you might find that some tasks need to be rearranged. You can easily move tasks from one row to another, either by cutting and pasting them or by dragging them. When you rearrange tasks, Project automatically reschedules the task list.

To cut and paste a task in the task list:

1   Click a row number to select the entire row.
2   In the Clipboard group, click Cut.
3   Click the row number below where you want to insert the cut task.
4   In the Clipboard group, click Paste.

To drag a task in the task list:

1   Click the row number to select the entire row. (Or drag across row numbers to select multiple sequential tasks.)
2   Drag the selected row to a new position in the task list.

You can use the Undo command to reverse changes in the order in which you made them. If you click the Undo button enough times, your project file will return to the state it was in when you last saved the file.

Do it!

B-2:   Rearranging tasks

Here's how	Here's why
1 Click **3**	To select the entire row for the task "Get approvals." You'll move this task to row 2.
2 Drag up between rows 1 and 2, as shown	 To move the task to row 2.
3 Observe the task list	"Get approvals" is now task 2, and the remaining tasks are renumbered automatically.
4 Scroll down to view the tasks at the bottom of the list	
5 Point to **23**, and drag down to 24	(Drag over the task numbers.) To select tasks 23 and 24, from the task number column, so that you can move both tasks.
6 Drag the selected tasks between 28 and 29, as shown	 To move the two tasks.
7 Save your changes	

Formatting the Sheet pane

Explanation

You can format the Sheet pane to suit your preferences and the specific project you're working on. For example, you can change the font and font size. You can also highlight specific tasks by applying a background color, or increase the width of the Sheet pane to view more columns.

Do it!

B-3: Formatting the task list

Here's how	Here's why
1 Click as shown	To select the entire Sheet pane.
2 In the Font group, click as shown	To open the Font list.
Scroll up and select **Arial**	To change the font to Arial.
3 Click as shown	To open the Font Size list.
Select **9**	To decrease the font size.
4 Point to the border between the Sheet pane and the Chart pane	The pointer changes to indicate that you can move the border in either direction.
5 Drag the border to the right until the Start and Finish columns are visible	To display more of the task information.
6 Save and close the project file	

Topic C: The Work Breakdown Structure

Explanation

The task list is called a *Work Breakdown Structure (WBS)*. The task ID numbers represent the WBS. The project summary task is the highest level of the WBS, and the other tasks are broken down to their lowest manageable levels. The WBS helps you to visualize the entire project in terms of scope, cost, time, and resources.

Summary tasks and subtasks

A *summary task* can be the overall objective of your project, or it can represent one of many major phases in a project. For example, a project summary task, the highest level of the work breakdown structure, might be "Build a house." Summary tasks representing major phases within this work breakdown structure might be "Install utilities" or "Lay foundation." A project can have as many summary tasks as needed to define a work breakdown structure.

Tasks that fall under a summary task are called *subtasks*. A summary task must contain subtasks that represent the activities needed to complete the summary task. If you delete or move a summary task, all of its subtasks are deleted or moved along with it.

Creating project summary tasks

To create a project summary task, click the Format tab and check Project Summary Task. This adds a summary task, with a default name taken from the project's file name, and gives it a task ID of 0. To rename the project summary task, select the name and type a new name.

Here's another way to create a project summary task: At the top of the task list, include the task that you want to be the project summary. Click the Task Name column heading to select all tasks in the list. Then, on the Task tab, click the Indent button. This indents all tasks except the first task in the list, thus establishing the highest-level task, the project summary task. This method does not set the project summary task ID to 0.

By default, all summary tasks are formatted with bold text in the Sheet pane. In the Chart pane, a summary task is represented by a gray bar that spans the duration of its subtasks, as shown in Exhibit 2-1.

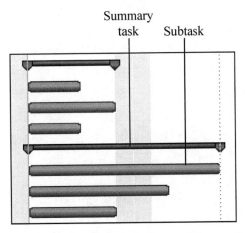

Exhibit 2-1: Summary tasks and their subtasks

Do it!

C-1: Creating a project summary task

The files for this activity are in Student Data folder **Unit 2\Topic C**.

Here's how	Here's why
1 Open Construction 2	
Save the file as **My Construction 2**	
2 Click the **Format** tab	
3 Check **Project Summary Task**	(In the Show/Hide group.) Project inserts a summary task at the top of the task list.
Observe the ID number	Project assigns the number zero to the project summary task.
Observe the task name	The default task name is taken from the file name. The text for a summary task is bold.
Observe the duration of the project summary task	The estimated duration is set to equal the current longest task duration in the project (3 weeks, or 15 work days.)
4 Observe the other tasks	They are indented below the summary task, because they are all subtasks of the project summary task.
5 Observe the Chart pane	The summary task appears as a gray bar that spans the length of the project.
6 Click **My Construction**	To select the summary task name.
Type **Build New Office** and press ⏎ ENTER	To rename the project summary task.
7 Save your changes	

Adding summary tasks

Explanation   There are two ways to create summary tasks for your major project phases. You can click the Summary button in the Insert group on the Task tab. This inserts a summary task, with default text, above the task that's selected in the Sheet pane. You can also create a full list of tasks and then use indenting and outdenting to establish the structure.

Indenting and outdenting tasks

Indenting and outdenting tasks is a critical part of establishing the WBS. When you indent a task, you move it one level down in the task hierarchy, and the task that precedes it becomes its summary task. To indent a task, select it and click the Indent button on the Task tab.

Moving a task up a level in the hierarchy is called *outdenting*. To outdent a task, select it and click the Outdent button on the Task tab. When you outdent a task, subsequent tasks become its subtasks.

Hiding and showing subtasks

You can collapse subtasks under their summary tasks to focus the task list on your main project phases. When you create a summary task, a small box with either a plus sign or a minus sign is displayed to the left of the summary task name, as shown in Exhibit 2-2. A minus sign indicates that the summary task is expanded; all of its subtasks are visible. A plus sign indicates that the subtasks are hidden. Clicking a plus sign expands the summary task to reveal its subtasks, while clicking a minus sign hides its subtasks.

You can also hide or show all subtasks simultaneously. On the View tab, click Outline. Then choose either Hide Subtasks or Show Subtasks.

If your task outline is complex and contains several levels of summary tasks, you can choose to hide only certain levels in the outline. On the View tab, click Outline and then choose Outline Level 2, Outline Level 3, and so on. If you choose Outline Level 1, only the project summary task is displayed. At Outline Level 2, the project summary task and all tasks directly beneath it are displayed, while subtasks deeper in the hierarchy are hidden, as shown in Exhibit 2-2.

Task Name	Duration	Start	Finish
⊟ **Project summary**	**11 days**	**Mon 5/3/10**	**Mon 5/17/10**
⊟ **Phase 1 summary**	**5 days**	**Mon 5/3/10**	**Fri 5/7/10**
subtask 1.1	3 days	Mon 5/3/10	Wed 5/5/10
subtask 1.2	5 days	Mon 5/3/10	Fri 5/7/10
subtask 1.3	3 days	Mon 5/3/10	Wed 5/5/10
⊟ **Phase 2 summary**	**9 days**	**Mon 5/3/10**	**Thu 5/13/10**
subtask 2.1	9 days	Mon 5/3/10	Thu 5/13/10
subtask 2.2	6 days	Mon 5/3/10	Mon 5/10/10
subtask 2.3	5 days	Mon 5/3/10	Fri 5/7/10
⊟ **Phase 3 summary**	**11 days**	**Mon 5/3/10**	**Mon 5/17/10**
⊞ **summary 1**	**5 days**	**Mon 5/3/10**	**Fri 5/7/10**
⊞ **summary 2**	**11 days**	**Mon 5/3/10**	**Mon 5/17/10**

Exhibit 2-2: A WBS, with some hidden subtasks

Hiding columns in the Sheet pane

Another way you can customize your view of a project is to hide columns that you don't need to use regularly. Doing so can make room for other columns and optimize your workspace for your specific project needs and your personal preferences. Hiding a column does not delete the information from the Project file; it merely conceals the information.

To hide a column, do either of the following:

- Right-click the column heading and choose Hide Column.
- Click a column heading (to select the column) and press Delete.

If you want to add a column, right-click any column and choose Insert Column. Then select the desired column from the column heading list.

Do it!

C-2: Defining a work breakdown structure

Here's how	Here's why
1 Drag to select rows 2–6, as shown	
	You'll indent tasks to build a WBS.
On the Task tab, click	(The Indent Tasks button.) To indent the selected tasks one level.
2 Observe the task in row 2	"Pre-construction" is now a summary task, indented below "Build New Office," which is the project summary task. The subtasks of "Pre-construction" are all indented below it.
3 Observe the Chart pane	"Pre-construction" now has a summary task bar.
4 Drag to select tasks 9–16	
Indent the tasks	(Click the Indent Tasks button.) The selected tasks fall under the "Foundation" phase of the project.
5 Click as shown	
	To collapse all subtasks of the Foundation phase of the project. Doing so can help you to more easily view and navigate the Sheet pane.

6 Hide the subtasks under
   Pre-construction

   Observe the task numbers   ID numbers for collapsed tasks are not
                                               displayed.

7 Select tasks 18–22

   Indent the selected tasks   To make them subtasks of the summary task
                                               "External work."

   Hide the subtasks under "External
   work"

8 Scroll down so that the last task is   If necessary.
   visible in the Sheet pane

9 Make tasks 24, 25, and 26   Select tasks 24–26, and click the Indent Tasks
   subtasks of "Distribute utilities"   button.

   Hide the subtasks under
   "Distribute utilities"

10 Select tasks 27–34

11 Click ⟦🚚 Summary⟧   (In the Insert group on the Task tab.) To insert a
                                               new summary task above the selection.

    Type **Internal work** and   To name the summary task. The selected tasks
    press ⟮↵ ENTER⟯   are already indented beneath it.

12 Click the **View** tab

    Click **Outline** and select   To show all subtasks in the task outline.
    All Subtasks

13 Right-click **Task Mode**   (The column heading at the top of the Sheet
                                               pane.) You'll hide this column because you will
                                               predominantly use automatic scheduling.

    Choose **Hide Column**   To hide the Task Mode column and create more
                                               space for the columns you'll be working with
                                               most often.

14 Save your changes

Milestone tasks

Explanation

In a typical project, you'll want to identify tasks that represent the completion of a major project phase or activity. These tasks are called *milestones;* each milestone is checkpoint in the life cycle of a project. Milestones have a duration of zero, and they are represented by black diamonds in the Gantt chart.

To insert a milestone task, click the Milestone button in the Insert group on the Task tab and then enter the milestone details. If a blank row is selected in the Sheet pane when you click Milestone, the milestone task is inserted at that location. If an existing task is selected, the milestone is inserted above that task.

You can also convert an existing task to a milestone. To do so:

1 In the Sheet pane, double-click the task to open the Task Information dialog box.
2 Click the Advanced tab.
3 Enter zero as the task duration, and check "Mark task as milestone."
4 Click OK.

Do it!

C-3: Setting milestones

Here's how	Here's why
1 Double-click **Building permit**	(Task 7.) To open the Task Information dialog box. You'll make this task a milestone.
Click the **Advanced** tab	If necessary.
2 In the Duration box, enter **0**	
Check **Mark task as milestone**	To designate this task as a milestone.
Click **OK**	To apply the settings and close the dialog box.
3 Observe the milestone in the Chart pane	Milestones are represented by black diamonds in the Chart pane. The date of a milestone is displayed next to it.
4 Scroll down to select task 36	
Set the task as a milestone	Double-click the task. On the Advanced tab of the Task Information dialog box, set the duration to zero and check "Mark task as milestone."
5 Click below Certificate of Occupancy	You'll add a new milestone task here.
Click ◆ Milestone	(In the Insert group of the Task tab.) To insert a new milestone task in the empty row.
Type **Office building complete** and press ↵ ENTER	The task duration is automatically set to 0 days.
6 Save your changes	

Gantt Chart styles

Explanation

Using the Format tab, you can quickly change Gantt Chart styles. When you're in Gantt Chart view, the Format tab displays several color schemes. Simply click an icon to apply the corresponding Gantt Chart style.

Custom bar styles

You can use the Bar Styles dialog box to further customize task bars. On the Format tab, click Format and choose Bar Styles. Select the chart element you want to format, such as Summary or Milestone. Select the desired shape, color, and pattern, and click OK.

Gridlines

Sometimes it can be hard to see which task bar corresponds to its task in the Sheet pane. Gridlines make it easier to associate tasks in the Sheet pane with their task bars in the Chart pane. When you select a task in the Sheet pane, its cell borders extend through the Chart pane, making it easier to see which task bar corresponds to that task.

To apply gridlines, click the Format tab, click Gridlines, and choose Gridlines. In the Gridlines dialog box, select an option from the "Line to change" list, select a line style from the Type list, select an interval if necessary, and click OK. You can also apply color to gridlines by selecting a color from the Color list.

C-4: Applying Gantt Chart styles

Here's how	Here's why
1 Scroll to the top of the task list	
Select any task	
2 Click the **Format** tab	
Observe the Gantt Chart Style group	You can click a Gantt Chart style to change the color scheme of the Gantt bars.
Click the gray chart style	
Switch to the orange chart style	
3 Click **Gridlines** and choose **Gridlines...**	To open the Gridlines dialog box.
In the "Line to change" list, verify that **Gantt Rows** is selected	
From the Type list, select the straight line at the top	
Click **OK**	To apply the gridlines. Notice that the selected task's cell borders extend through the Chart pane, making it easier to identify the task's corresponding task bar.
4 Change the gridline style to a dotted line	Click Gridlines and choose Gridlines. Select the dotted line from the Type list and click OK.
5 Save and close the project file	

Unit summary: Tasks

Topic A   In this topic, you learned how to create a **task list** in user-controlled scheduling mode and automatic scheduling mode. You also learned how to set task **durations** and set the default scheduling mode for all new files.

Topic B   In this topic, you learned how to **modify a task list** by adding and deleting tasks. You also learned how to rearrange tasks and format the information in the Sheet pane.

Topic C   In this topic, you learned how to establish a project's **Work Breakdown Structure (WBS)**—the task hierarchy or outline. You learned how to create a project summary task, phase summary tasks, and subtasks. Then, you learned how to hide and show subtasks, hide columns in the Sheet pane, insert milestone tasks, and apply Gantt Chart styles.

Independent practice activity

In this activity, you'll enter task information, delete and move tasks, create summary tasks, and hide and show subtasks.

The files for this activity are in Student Data folder **Unit 2\Unit summary**.

1 Open Office Construction.

2 Save the file as **My Office Construction**.

3 Set the project to start one month from today's date.

4 Insert a project summary task named **Build new office**. (*Hint*: Click the Format tab.)

5 Make tasks 9–15 subtasks of "Foundation." (*Hint:* Click the Task tab.)

6 Move the task **Lay slab foundation** above the task **Foundation walls**.

7 Make task 7 ("Building permit") a milestone task.

8 Scroll down to the bottom of the task list and add a new milestone as the last task. Name the milestone **Office building complete**.

9 Select the new milestone and make it *not* a part of the "Internal work" summary task. (*Hint:* On the Task tab, click Outdent Task.)

10 Hide the subtasks under the "Distribute Utilities" and "Internal work" summary tasks.

11 Save and close the project file.

Review questions

1 In what circumstances might user-controlled scheduling be helpful to you?

2 True or false? If you want to specify that a task's duration is two weeks, simply enter 2 in the Duration column for that task.

3 True or false? When you rearrange tasks, Project automatically reschedules the task list.

4 The task hierarchy or outline is called which of the following?

   A The list

   B The Work Breakdown Structure

   C The project pyramid

   D The project summary task

5 True or false? You can establish the WBS by entering all of your tasks and then indenting and outdenting them to establish the structure.

6 What is a milestone?

Unit 3

Task scheduling

Unit time: 75 minutes

Complete this unit, and you'll know how to:

A Establish a project schedule by linking tasks, modifying task predecessors, setting lag time and lead time, and adding recurring tasks.

B Work in Network Diagram view and modify task relationships.

C Apply different task types and set task constraints.

Topic A: Task links

Explanation
Scheduling refers to the timing and sequencing of tasks. As a project manager, you'll need to schedule tasks to complete your project on time. As you enter tasks and other related information in the task list, Project automatically schedules each task on the basis of the project start date (with the exception of any tasks that are set to manual scheduling).

Tasks in a project are often related, so it's important to sequence them according to their relationships. To do this, you link the tasks. After you link tasks, you might need to make adjustments, such as modifying dependencies or unlinking some tasks.

Dependencies

Tasks are scheduled based on the project's start date (specified in the Project Information dialog box) and the task's duration. In real life, however, not all tasks start on the same date. For example, if you're building a house, you can't install a roof on the same day that you lay the foundation. There are *dependencies* between tasks that define the way in which tasks are related or linked.

When you link tasks, Project automatically applies a Finish-to-Start task dependency so that the start of the second task is dependent on the completion of the first task. For example, the task "Plan office layout" must be completed before the task "Begin construction" can start.

The predecessor-successor link

When you link tasks, the task that starts or finishes before the other task can begin is called a *predecessor* task. A task that cannot start or finish until the start or completion of a previous task is called a *successor* task.

To link tasks, select them and click the Link Tasks button on the Task tab. (You can also select the tasks and press Ctrl+F2.) When you link tasks, blue arrows link the task bars in the Chart pane, helping you to visualize the scheduling relationship between the tasks.

Unlinking tasks

When you unlink tasks, Project schedules them to start on the same day by default. Sometimes you can do this to shorten the duration of your project. Suppose, for example, that after linking all tasks, you determine that the tasks "Get approvals" and "Select architects" can be done independently and can run in parallel. Therefore, you can unlink them.

To unlink tasks, select them and click the Unlink Tasks button on the Task tab.

Temporary highlighting of changes

When you make changes that affect the schedule, Project highlights all of the fields in the Sheet pane that are affected by the change. The highlighting allows you to verify your changes and see how your actions affect task schedules. This highlighting goes away when you save your changes or when you make further changes in the project file.

Do it!

A-1: Linking and unlinking tasks

The files for this activity are in Student Data folder **Unit 3\Topic A**.

Here's how	Here's why
1 Open New office	
Save the file as **My New office**	
2 Set the project to start one month from today	On the Project tab, click Project Information. Set the start date and click OK.
3 Select tasks 2–7	
	You'll link these tasks so that Project schedules them in sequence.
On the Task tab, click	(In the Schedule group.) To establish links between the selected tasks.
4 Observe the highlighted cells in the Sheet pane	All cells that are affected by linking tasks 2 through 7 are temporarily highlighted in blue.
Observe the Start and Finish dates	Because these tasks must now be done in sequence, Project automatically revises the task schedules.
Observe the Predecessors field	This field shows which tasks (by number) are predecessors of another task. For example, task 5 shows that task 4 is a predecessor because you can't review the blueprint until the architect has drawn the plans.
5 In the status bar, click two times where shown	
	To zoom out so you can see the linked tasks.
6 Observe the Chart pane	
	The arrows indicate task links.

7 In the Sheet pane, select task 7

   Press CTRL | You'll select a non-contiguous range of tasks.

   Drag to select tasks 9–16

7		Building permit
8		⊟ **Foundation**
9		Survey and stake
10		Excavate for found
11		Footings
12		Install drainage
13		Install external utiliti
14		Foundation walls
15		Lay slab foundatior
16		Backfill

To select task 7 and tasks 9 through 16 simultaneously.

   Release CTRL

   Click 🔗 | (In the Schedule group.) To link these non-contiguous tasks. The task schedules are updated.

8 Observe the Start and Finish dates | Project automatically schedules the tasks according to their duration and task relationships.

9 Select tasks 2 and 3 | In the Task Name column.

10 Click 🔗 | (In the Schedule group.) To unlink tasks 2 and 3.

   Observe the Start field | The two tasks now begin on the same date.

   Observe the Gantt chart | In the Gantt chart, the two task bars are aligned under the same start date.

11 Save and close the file

Changing predecessors

Explanation

You might need to change the predecessor of a task to make better use of time and resources. For example, consider the following short series of tasks: erect external walls; install siding; and install roof. The task "Install roof" can start as soon as the task "Erect external walls" is completed, and it does not depend on its immediate predecessor task, "Install siding."

Thus, you can change the predecessor of the task "Install roof" to "Erect external walls." To do so, simply change the value in the Predecessors field to the task ID that you want to set as the predecessor.

You can also use the Task Information dialog box. Here's how:

1 In the Sheet pane, double-click the task whose predecessor you want to change. This opens the Task Information dialog box.

2 Click the Predecessors tab.

3 In the ID column, enter the task ID of the task that you want to set as the predecessor.

4 Click OK.

Do it!

A-2: Changing task predecessors

The files for this activity are in Student Data folder **Unit 3\Topic A**.

Here's how	Here's why
1 Open New project	
Save the file as **My New project**	
2 Set the project to start one month from today	
3 Observe task 22	(Install roof.) The roof is scheduled to be installed after the siding is installed (task 21). However, the roof installation does not depend on the siding. It depends only on erecting the external walls.
4 Click the Predecessors field for task 22	
Type **19** and press (← ENTER)	To specify task 19 (Erect external walls) as the only predecessor for this task. Now, after the external walls are erected, the task of installing the roof can begin.
5 Observe the Predecessor field for task 24	Task 22 (Install roof) is listed as the only predecessor for task 24 (Frame internal walls). However, the project team decides that the windows and external doors should be installed before the framing of internal walls begins.
In the Predecessor field, click to the right of 22	22
	Task 20 (Install windows, external doors) must be completed before task 24 can begin.
Type **,20** and press (← ENTER)	(A comma, followed by 20.) To make tasks 22 and 20 predecessors of task 24.
6 Save your changes	

Lag time and lead time

Explanation

In your task list, you might have a task that can start before the completion of its predecessor. In such cases, you can reschedule your tasks and thereby complete them earlier. You can apply lag time or lead time to a task's predecessor. *Lag time* is a delay that adds time after the completion of a task. For example, consider the task "Install trim." If you add lag time to its predecessor, "Paint," you can be sure the paint will have time to dry before the installation of the trim begins.

Lead time is overlap between dependent tasks. Sometimes a task can start before its predecessor finishes. For example, when a task such as "Install trim" is 75% complete, you might determine that the next task, "Install built-in amenities," can begin. Therefore, you can set 25% lead time to the task "Install built-in amenities."

Applying lag time or lead time

To apply lag time or lead time, double-click a task in the Sheet pane to open the Task Information dialog box. Click the Predecessors tab to view the task's predecessor(s). To apply lag time, enter a positive value in the Lag field for the predecessor and click OK. To set lead time, enter a negative value. Using the previous example, you would enter -25% in the Lag field.

You can also double-click the link line between task bars in the Chart pane. This opens the Task Dependency dialog box. Enter a value in the Lag box and click OK.

Do it!

A-3: Adding lead time and lag time to tasks

Here's how	Here's why
1 Scroll down and select task 32	The "Install trim" task.
Click	(In the Editing group.) So that Gantt Chart view scrolls to the selected task.
Observe the start date	Task 32 begins after task 31 is finished.
2 Double-click task 32	To open the Task Information dialog box.
Click the **Predecessors** tab	"Paint" is listed as the only predecessor of task 32.
In the Lag box, enter **1**	To add one day of lag time.
Click **OK**	There is now one day of lag between the end of task 31 and the start of task 32. This will give the paint a chance to dry before the trim is installed.
3 Observe the Predecessors field for task 32	The predecessor is task 31, its type is Finish-to-Start (FS), and there is now one day of lag time.
4 Double-click **Install furnishings**	(Task 34.) You'll add lead time to this task because it can begin before its predecessor task is finished.
On the Predecessors tab, in the Lag field, enter **-50%**	Lead time is negative lag time. This change ensures that task 34 can begin before task 33 is completed. Be sure to include the percent sign, or Project will schedule this as -50 days.
Click **OK**	To close the dialog box.

5 Observe the link line	
	This overlapping indicates lead time—the task "Install furnishings" starts when its predecessor is 50% complete.
6 Observe the Predecessors field for task 34	It shows task 33 as the predecessor, with a Finish-to-Start relationship and 50% lead time.
7 Save your changes	

Recurring tasks

Explanation

Tasks that occur at regular intervals during the course of a project are called *recurring tasks*. For example, to monitor the progress of your project, you might want to conduct review meetings at regular intervals.

The Sheet pane displays a recurring task as a summary task consisting of subtasks. A Recurring Task icon appears in the Indicators field, next to the summary task. For each recurring task, task bars appear at regular intervals in the Chart pane.

To insert a recurring task:

1 In the Task Name field, select the cell below where you want to insert a recurring task.

2 In the Insert group on the Task tab, click the Task button's arrow and choose Recurring Task to open the Recurring Task Information dialog box.

3 In the Task Name box, enter a name for the recurring task.

4 In the Duration box, enter the duration.

5 Under Recurrence pattern, select the time interval.

6 Under Range of recurrence, in the Start and End by lists, enter the dates across which the recurring task will occur.

7 From the Calendar list, select the calendar you want to use for scheduling the recurring task.

8 Click OK.

Do it!

A-4:   Adding recurring tasks

Here's how	Here's why
1 Scroll up to select task 1	You'll insert a new row above this row to add recurring task information.
Click **Scroll to Task**	In the Editing group on the Task tab.

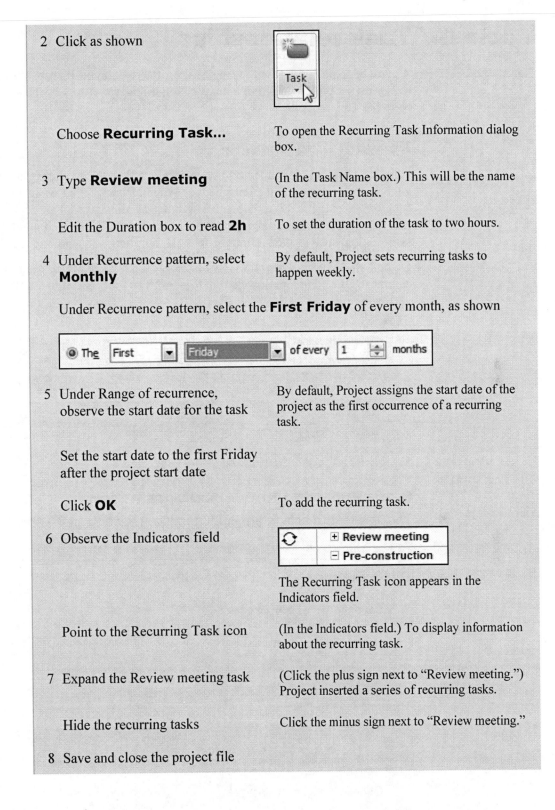

2 Click as shown

Choose **Recurring Task...** — To open the Recurring Task Information dialog box.

3 Type **Review meeting** — (In the Task Name box.) This will be the name of the recurring task.

Edit the Duration box to read **2h** — To set the duration of the task to two hours.

4 Under Recurrence pattern, select **Monthly** — By default, Project sets recurring tasks to happen weekly.

Under Recurrence pattern, select the **First Friday** of every month, as shown

5 Under Range of recurrence, observe the start date for the task — By default, Project assigns the start date of the project as the first occurrence of a recurring task.

Set the start date to the first Friday after the project start date

Click **OK** — To add the recurring task.

6 Observe the Indicators field

The Recurring Task icon appears in the Indicators field.

Point to the Recurring Task icon — (In the Indicators field.) To display information about the recurring task.

7 Expand the Review meeting task — (Click the plus sign next to "Review meeting.") Project inserted a series of recurring tasks.

Hide the recurring tasks — Click the minus sign next to "Review meeting."

8 Save and close the project file

Topic B: Task relationships

Explanation

As you become familiar with using Microsoft Project, you'll probably develop your own viewing preferences. For example, you might prefer to view task information in Network Diagram view.

Network Diagram view

Network Diagram view displays the project as a flowchart to help you visualize and analyze task details and the links between them. Boxes called *nodes* represent tasks. Lines connect the nodes to indicate task links. Summary tasks are represented by parallelograms, and subtasks are represented by rectangles. Each node displays task information, such as the task name, task ID, duration, and start and finish dates.

By default, Network Diagram view displays each node at 100% zoom. However, you cannot see the complete flowchart at this level, so you'll need to scroll horizontally and vertically.

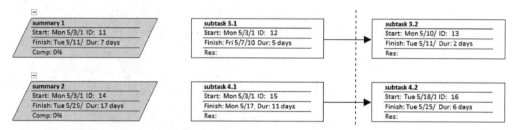

Exhibit 3-1: Nodes in Network Diagram view

Do it!

B-1: Exploring Network Diagram view

The files for this activity are in Student Data folder **Unit 3\Topic B**.

Here's how	Here's why
1 Open Project 2	
Save the file as **My Project 2**	
2 Select **Pre-construction**	You'll view this summary task in Network Diagram view.
3 Click as shown	
Choose **Network Diagram**	To switch to Network Diagram view. This view displays information in the form of a flowchart.

4	Locate the summary tasks	Summary tasks are represented by parallelograms.
	In the status bar, click where shown	
		To see more of the tasks. They are represented by boxes (nodes). Arrows represent the links between them.
5	Locate the subtasks	A rectangle represents a subtask.
6	On the View tab, click as shown	
	Choose **Zoom...**	To open the Zoom dialog box.
	Select **50%** and click **OK**	
7	Point to any node	To enlarge the task node for easier reading.
8	Observe the dashed lines	These indicate page breaks to help you see how a printout would paginate.
9	On the Zoom slider, click as shown	
		To zoom in to the middle of the range.
10	Click the **Format** tab	
	Click **Collapse Boxes**	To display only the task IDs in boxes for a big-picture view of the flowchart.
11	Point to any node	Even with the boxes collapsed, you can point to a node to display task details.
	Click **Collapse Boxes**	To return to the default node formatting.
12	Save your changes	

Modifying task relationships

Explanation

Network Diagram view provides an alternate way to view the links and dependencies between tasks. As you review task relationships, you might find that some tasks do not actually depend on each other as indicated in the schedule. You can reschedule tasks by modifying the task links. (You can do this in Gantt Chart view and Network Diagram view.) When you modify a task relationship, Project automatically recalculates the project schedule.

Task relationships

When you link tasks, you can establish different task relationships, depending on the circumstances. The dependencies you use will affect the project schedule. By default, Project assigns a Finish-to-Start link. If two tasks can run concurrently, you can apply a Start-to-Start dependency.

The following table describes the available task dependencies and shows how each dependency is displayed in a Gantt chart.

Dependency	Gantt bar example	Description
Finish-to-Start (FS)		Task B cannot start unless Task A is finished.
Start-to-Start (SS)		Task B cannot start unless Task A starts.
Finish-to-Finish (FF)		Task B cannot finish unless Task A is finished.
Start-to-Finish (SF)		Task B cannot finish unless Task A starts.

To modify a task dependency, double-click the link line to open the Task Dependency dialog box, shown in Exhibit 3-2. From the Type list, select the type of task relationship you want to use. Then click OK.

Exhibit 3-2: The Task Dependency dialog box

Scrolling the Chart pane

Perhaps the easiest way to navigate the Chart pane is to use the new Timeline. If you want to see more of the Chart pane, you can drag the edge of the Timeline to the right so that more calendar days are visible. This compresses the Gantt bars, but they retain their relative sizes.

You can also use the Timeline to scroll to view specific tasks. When you point to the horizontal bar above the Timeline, it turns dark blue. Drag it to the left or right to scroll the Chart pane.

The Go To dialog box

When you have a long task list, it can sometimes be difficult to find a particular task, especially if you're working in Network Diagram view. You can use the Go To dialog box to quickly jump to a task. To do so, press F5 or Ctrl+G, enter the task ID or date you want to see, and click OK.

Critical tasks

Critical tasks are tasks that must be completed on schedule for a project to be finished on time. By monitoring the critical tasks in your project and the resources assigned to those tasks, you can determine which tasks are affecting your project's finish date and thereby devise a contingency plan if necessary. In Network Diagram view, critical tasks are shown in red. Tasks that are not critical remain blue by default.

The sequence of critical tasks is called the *critical path*, and it's dynamic. It changes as tasks are completed or delayed or when dependencies between tasks are changed.

B-2:   Changing task relationships

Here's how	Here's why
1 Press ⟨CTRL⟩ + ⟨G⟩	To open the Go To dialog box. This is a fast way to go directly to a specific task, particularly in Network Diagram view.
Type **10** and click **OK**	To go to and select task 10 (Select architect). It's red, indicating that it's a critical task; if it's delayed, it will affect the project finish date.
2 Observe task 9	(Get approvals.) This task is not currently a critical task. You'll link task 9 to task 10.
3 Drag from the middle of task 9 to task 10	To create a link between these tasks in Network Diagram view. Task 9 is now red, indicating that it's a critical task—any delay in the completion of this task can affect the project finish date.
Observe the dates of the tasks	"Select architect" is scheduled to start after "Get approvals" is finished. You want to change this task relationship.
4 Double-click the link line between the two tasks	To open the Task Dependency dialog box. You can also click link lines in Gantt Chart view to open this dialog box.
Observe the Type box	By default, Project links tasks with a Finish-to-Start (FS) relationship.
5 From the Type list, select **Start-to-Start (SS)**, and click **OK**	To schedule tasks 9 and 10 to run in parallel. The start dates of the two tasks are now the same.
6 Scroll to the right to view task 11	If necessary.
Drag from the middle of task 9 to the middle of task 11	To create a link between tasks 9 and 11, because the architect cannot begin drawing plans until everything is approved.
7 Observe the new link line between tasks 9 and 11	
	Task 11 (Draw plans) now depends on the completion of task 9 (Get approvals).
8 Click the **Task** tab	
9 Switch to Gantt Chart view	
Select task 9	
Click **Scroll to task**	

10 Click the **View** tab

   Click **Zoom** and choose **Zoom...**   In Gantt Chart view, the zoom options are provided in units of time.

   Select **1 month** and click **OK**   To view one month of time in the Chart pane.

11 In the Timeline, point as shown

   The pointer changes to indicate that you can drag in either direction.

   Drag to the right, past March   To expand the Timeline to display all Pre-construction subtasks.

12 Observe the task bars and link lines for tasks 9, 10, and 11

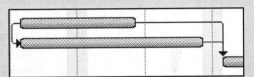

   Tasks 9 and 10 have the same start date because of their new dependency.

13 In the Timeline, point as shown

   Drag to the right   As you drag the Timeline, the task bars for the highlighted period come into view. This is an efficient way to navigate your project.

14 Save and close the project file

Topic C: Task options

Explanation

So far, you've learned how to plan a project by creating a task list, linking tasks, and defining task dependencies. To manage your project efficiently and effectively, you also need to set task types and constraints.

Task types

There are three general task types: Fixed Duration, Fixed Work, and Fixed Unit.

Task type	Description
Fixed Duration	A *Fixed Duration* task has a constant time value. Even if you increase the resources allocated to the task, the duration will remain the same. For example, say that a task has a fixed duration of two days, and two resources are assigned to it. Even if another resource is added to the task, Project will not change the duration.
Fixed Work	In a *Fixed Work* task, the total work to be performed has a constant value. The total amount of work performed on a task is the sum of resources used on that task. For example, if three resources work an eight-hour schedule for two days, the total work performed on the task is 48 hours (3 resources multiplied by 8 hours multiplied by 2 days). Therefore, the task has a fixed work value of 48 hours.
Fixed Unit	A *Fixed Unit* task has a constant quantity or units-of-resource value. For example, tasks that require wood or paint are fixed-unit tasks because such resources remain constant, regardless of any change in task duration.

Do it!

C-1: Changing a task type

The files for this activity are in Student Data folder **Unit 3\Topic C**.

Here's how	Here's why
1 Open Work project	
Save the file as **My Work project**	
2 Double-click **Get approvals**	To open the Task Information dialog box. You'll mark this task as a Fixed Duration task.
3 Click the **Advanced** tab	
From the Task type list, select **Fixed Duration**	To make this a fixed-duration task. No matter how many resources are assigned to this task, it will still take two weeks to complete.
Click **OK**	To apply the settings.
4 Save your changes	

Task constraints

Explanation

Constraints are limitations imposed on tasks. When planning a project, you need to be aware of external factors such as deadlines and the availability of resources. You can set task constraints to control the start and finish dates of a task. Task constraints affect a project's schedule, duration, and flexibility.

The following table describes the task constraints you can apply.

Constraint	Description
As Late As Possible	Schedules a task to start as late as possible. Project schedules a task with this constraint from the finish date of the project.
As Soon As Possible	Schedules a task to begin as early as possible. This is the default task constraint when you schedule a task from the start date of the project.
Finish No Earlier Than	Schedules a task to finish on or after a specified date. A task with this constraint cannot finish before the specified date.
Finish No Later Than	Schedules a task to finish on or before a specified date. A task with this constraint cannot finish after the specified date.
Must Finish On	Schedules a task to finish on the specified date.
Must Start On	Schedules a task to start on a specified date.
Start No Earlier Than	Schedules a task to start on or after a specified date.
Start No Later Than	Schedules a task to start on or before a specified date.

Do it!

C-2: Applying task constraints

Here's how	Here's why
1 Scroll down and double-click **Office building complete**	(The project completion milestone.) You'll set a constraint for this task.
Verify that the Advanced tab is active	
2 Observe the Constraint type box	Project assigns the constraint As Soon As Possible to tasks by default.
From the Constraint type list, select **Finish No Later Than**	To set the project to finish no later than a specified date.
3 In the Constraint date box, enter **7/6/12**	To specify the last date on which the project can finish.
Click **OK**	To close the dialog box.
4 Select any empty cell below the selected task	To deselect task 44.
Observe the Indicators field	A Task Constraint icon is displayed for task 44.
Point to the Task Constraint icon	A ScreenTip appears, showing details of the constraint set for this task.
5 Save and close the project file	

Unit summary: Task scheduling

Topic A   In this topic, you learned how to establish a schedule by **linking tasks**. You learned about **task dependencies**, and you learned how to link and unlink tasks. You learned how to change task predecessors to fine-tune a schedule, and how to set lag time and lead time. Finally, you learned how to insert **recurring tasks**.

Topic B   In this topic, you learned how to work in **Network Diagram view**. You learned how to link tasks in this view and **modify task relationships**. You also learned how to use the Go To dialog box to go directly to a task, and how to navigate a Gantt chart by using the **Timeline**.

Topic C   In this topic, you learned about the three **task types**: Fixed Duration, Fixed Work, and Fixed Unit. You also learned about various **task constraints** and how to apply them.

Independent practice activity

In this activity, you'll link and unlink tasks, change the predecessor of a task, and add lag time to a task. You'll also create a recurring task, change the relationship type between tasks, and assign a constraint to a task.

The files for this activity are in Student Data folder **Unit 3\Unit summary**.

1 Open Work project 2.

2 Save the file as **My Work project 2**.

3 Link tasks 18 through 22.

4 Unlink tasks 31 and 35. (*Hint:* Press and hold Ctrl to select both tasks.)

5 Change the predecessor of task 22 to task 20.

6 Add a lag time of two days after task 19 (Erect external walls).

7 Add **Weekly status** as a recurring task above Pre-construction. Set the duration to **1 hr**, and set it to occur once **weekly**, every **Monday**.

8 Switch to Network Diagram view. Use the Go To dialog box to jump to task **50**.

9 Create a Start-to-Start relationship between the tasks **Install siding** and **Install roof**.

10 Switch to Gantt Chart view.

11 Assign a Must Start On constraint to task 46 (Erect steel frame). Verify that the constraint date is **4/1/11**. Continue with the constraint, allowing any scheduling conflicts that might arise.

12 Save and close the project file.

Review questions

1 True or false? Tasks in a project are often related, so it's important to sequence them according to their relationships.

2 True or false? Dependencies between tasks define the way in which tasks are related or linked.

3 What is lag time?

4 How do you link tasks?

5 True or false? To modify task relationships, you need to use Network Diagram view.

6 Task B cannot start unless Task A is finished. This describes which of the following task dependencies?

   A Start-to-Start

   B Finish-to-Finish

   C Finish-to-Start

   D Start-to-Finish

7 Task B cannot finish unless Task A starts. This describes which of the following task dependencies?

   A Start-to-Start

   B Finish-to-Finish

   C Finish-to-Start

   D Start-to-Finish

8 Which of the following task constraints schedules a task to finish on or before a specified date?

   A Start No Earlier Than

   B Finish No Later Than

   C As Late As Possible

   D As Soon As Possible

Unit 4

Resource management

Unit time: 60 minutes

Complete this unit, and you'll know how to:

A Create a base calendar for a project and edit the working time.

B Create a resource pool and a resource calendar, assign resources to tasks, and create and apply a task calendar.

C Enter resource costs, and use the Cost table.

Topic A: The base calendar

Explanation

Project schedules tasks according to a base calendar. A *base calendar* defines the working days and working hours for a project. After you create a base calendar, you apply it to a project to establish the project's calendar.

Creating a base calendar

Every project is linked to a base calendar. Project provides three calendars: Standard, 24 Hour, and Night Shift. The Standard calendar is the default base calendar. It uses a Monday-through-Friday work week, working hours from 8 AM to 5 PM (with an hour off at noon), and no holidays. You can use any built-in calendar or create a base calendar of your own.

Every organization has its own working hours. If your organization's working and nonworking hours differ from the default hours of the base calendar, you can create a base calendar and apply it to the project. To plan your project accurately, you'll also need to specify any holidays that your company observes—the default base calendar does not include holidays.

When you designate a day as a working day, it applies to all months. When you designate a day as a *nonworking* day, it applies to only that month. Project then schedules all tasks, taking into account designated holidays and nonworking time.

To create a base calendar and apply it to a project:

1 On the Project tab, click Change Working Time to open the Change Working Time Dialog box, shown in Exhibit 4-1.
2 Click Create New Calendar to open the Create New Base Calendar dialog box.
3 In the Name box, type a name for the calendar.
4 Select "Create new base calendar" and click OK.
5 Make the necessary changes in the calendar in the Change Working Time dialog box.
6 Specify the calendar exceptions and working times for the work weeks.
7 Click OK to close the Change Working Time dialog box.
8 On the Ribbon, click Project Information.
9 From the Calendar list, select the base calendar you just created. Click OK.

When you save your project file, changes in the base calendar are also saved in the project file.

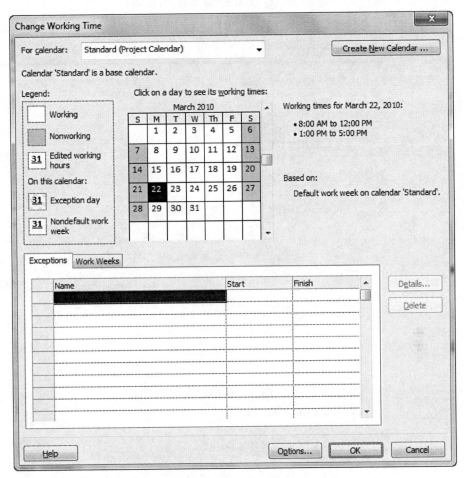

Exhibit 4-1: The Change Working Time dialog box

Do it!

A-1:   Creating a base calendar

The files for this activity are in Student Data folder **Unit 4\Topic A**.

Here's how	Here's why
1 Open Office project	You'll create a base calendar for the project that is specific to the company.
Save the project file as **My Office project**	
2 Click the **Project** tab	
Click **Change Working Time**	To open the Change Working Time dialog box. It displays the current month with default working times. Today's date is selected in the calendar.
3 In the calendar, click any nonworking day	(Nonworking days are shaded.) Nonworking days do not have working times listed to the right of the calendar.
4 Click **Create New Calendar**	To open the Create New Base Calendar dialog box.
Type **Outlander office construction**	(In the Name box.) To give the calendar a name.
Select **Create new base calendar**	
Click **OK**	To create a base calendar and return to the Change Working Time dialog box.
5 Observe the list box at the top of the dialog box	The name of the new base calendar is displayed.
6 To the right of the calendar, scroll down to view May 2012	
Click the box for Friday, May 25	To select it. You'll declare this a nonworking day because there is a company-wide picnic and holiday scheduled for that day.
7 On the Exceptions tab, click in the first column under Name	
Type **Company holiday** and press (↵ ENTER)	To name the exception in the calendar.
8 Observe the date in the Calendar	The date is highlighted to indicate that it's a nonworking day.
9 In the Calendar, select **28**	You'll specify a standard holiday as a nonworking day.

10	Click under Company holiday	(In the Name column of Row 2.) You'll name the nonworking day for May 28th.
	Type **Memorial Day** and press ⏎ ENTER	To declare this a nonworking day.
11	Scroll up to March 2012	
	Select **9**	You'll make Friday, March 9th a company-wide holiday.
	In the Name column, enter **Company holiday**	

	Name
1	Company holiday
2	Memorial Day
3	Company holiday

	Click **OK**	
12	Go to task 43	(Press Ctrl+G and enter 43, or scroll down.) This is the completion milestone.
	Observe the completion date	The project is set to be completed on 6/20. Now you'll apply the new project calendar and observe how it affects the completion date.
13	On the Project tab, click **Project Information**	To open the Project Information dialog box.
14	Observe the Calendar list box	The default calendar, Standard, is still applied to the project.
15	From the Calendar list, select **Outlander office construction**	This will be the new base calendar for the project.
	Click **OK**	To close the dialog box.
16	Observe the completion date	Project automatically updates the task dates to accommodate the nonworking days, resulting in a new completion date of 6/25.
17	Save and close the project file	

Topic B: Resources and calendars

Explanation

When you're a project manager, one of the main areas you need to focus on during the planning phase of a project is resource availability. You have to determine the resources (people, tools, equipment, and materials) and the quantity of each resource that will be required for the project. Based on availability, you assign resources to individual tasks to meet the goals and objectives of the project.

The resource pool

The list of resources needed to complete a project is called the *resource pool*. It is critical that you refer to the Work Breakdown Structure, project objectives, and organizational policies when you plan your resources. This helps you to effectively assign resources based on their skills, the project requirements, and project costs.

You can add work resources, cost resources, and material resources to your project plan. A *work resource* performs work on a task. Common examples of work resources are people and equipment. A *cost resource* is a fixed amount of money applied to a task without making the cost dependent on work performed. For example, storage facility costs and airfare are cost resources. A *material resource* is an item that's used to perform work on a task. Paint, wood, steel, and fuel are examples of material resources.

The Resource Sheet

You create a resource pool in Resource Sheet view, which resembles a spreadsheet with columns and rows. You can enter such information as resource name and type, material label, group, standard and overtime rates, cost, and the calendar the resource uses. You can review and edit information about any resource in Resource Sheet view.

The column headings indicate where to enter resource information. For example, enter a name in the Resource Name field. Enter the type of resource, such as work, material, or cost, in the Type field. Enter a unit of measurement—such as gallons, if the material is paint—in the Material Label field. (This field applies only to material resources, not to work or cost resources.) Use the Group field to specify a group, such as the department or category to which the resource belongs.

By default, the MaxUnits field displays 100%, which indicates the availability of a single resource and its working time. For example, if you have two excavators for your project, you specify 200% in the MaxUnits field. (This field applies only to work resources, not to material or cost resources.)

Resources and the base calendar

You assign a calendar to a work resource in the Base Calendar field. Project applies the Standard calendar to all work resources unless you first apply a new base calendar to the project by using the Project Information dialog box. (Base calendars do not apply to material or cost resources.)

Do it!

B-1: Creating a resource pool

The files for this activity are in Student Data folder **Unit 4\Topic B**.

Here's how	Here's why
1 Open Office project 2	
Save the file as **My Office project 2**	
2 In the status bar, click as shown	To switch to Resource Sheet view, which resembles a spreadsheet, with resource fields as column headings.
3 Select the first cell under Resource Name	
Type **Kathy Sinclair**	This will be the first resource name for the project.
Press (TAB)	To move to the next field.
Observe the Type field	By default, Project sets the resource type to Work and fills in several other default values.
Observe the Initials field	Project automatically provides an initial for the resource name.
4 In the Group field, type **MGMT**	(As an abbreviation for "management.") This resource will oversee the project.
5 In the Resource Name field, select the second cell	You'll add the details for a second resource.
Type **David James** and press (TAB)	This will be the second resource name.
In the Group field, type **CONST**	(As an abbreviation for "Construction.") This resource will be in the Construction group.
6 Select the third cell under Resource Name	
Type **Paint**	Resources can be anyone or anything needed to complete a project.
Press (TAB)	To move to the Type field.
7 From the Type list, select **Material**	To designate this resource as a material resource.

8 Double-click where shown	Material ▾✛itials ▾ Material Label
	To make the column width fit the full column heading. (Double-clicking the column border adjusts the column width to fit the widest cell in the column.)
In the Material Label field for Paint, type **gallons**	This is the unit of measurement for this resource.
In the Group field, type **Purchased**	
9 Add a new resource named **Airfare to Chicago**	
Set the resource type to **Cost**	Airfare is a cost resource.
In the Group field, type **Travel**	
10 Save and close the project file	

Resource calendars

Explanation

If you have created and applied a base calendar for your project before you start building your resource list, that calendar will automatically appear in the Base Calendar column for each work resource. However, if the working and nonworking times of your project calendar do not coincide with the availability of a resource, you can create a resource calendar. A *resource calendar* is specific to a particular resource. For example, a resource calendar might reflect a resource's personal vacation schedule.

To create a resource calendar:

1 In Resource Sheet view, in the Name field, select the resource to which you want to assign a calendar.
2 On the Resource tab, click Information to open the Resource Information dialog box.
3 Click Change Working Time to open the Change Working Time dialog box.
4 Make the necessary changes in the calendar and click OK.
5 Click OK.

Do it!   **B-2:   Creating a resource calendar**

The files for this activity are in Student Data folder **Unit 4\Topic B**.

Here's how	Here's why
1 Open Office project 3	This resource sheet contains complete information about the resources for the project. You'll create a resource calendar for one of the resources.
Save the file as **My Office project 3**	
2 In the Resource Name field, select **David James**	You'll change the calendar for this resource.
Click the **Resource** tab	
Click	To open the Resource Information dialog box.
3 Click **Change Working Time**	To open the Change Working Time dialog box.
4 Verify that **Outlander office construction** is selected	In the Base calendar list.
5 Scroll to the March 2012 calendar	(If necessary.) You'll set a nonworking day specifically for David because he has requested that day off.
6 Select **2**	You'll set March 2nd as a day off for David.
In the Name column, enter **Vacation day**	
Click **OK**	To apply the new resource calendar and return to the Resource Information dialog box.
Click **OK**	To close the dialog box.
7 Save your changes	

Assigning resources

Explanation

After you plan tasks and create the resource pool, you assign resources to complete those tasks. You assign resources to tasks in Gantt Chart view.

To assign resources:

1 Switch to Gantt Chart view.

2 Select the task to which you want to assign a resource.

3 On the Task tab, click Assign Resources to open the Assign Resources dialog box.

4 Select a resource and click Assign to assign the resource to the task.

5 Click Close.

You can also open the Assign Resources dialog box by selecting a task and pressing Alt+F10.

The resource graph

When you want to assign a resource to a task, you need to know the resource's availability. You can view the availability of resources by creating a resource graph. Tasks assigned to over-allocated resources can be reassigned to resources that are available. By using resource graphs, you can also compare the availability of different resources.

Do it!

B-3:   Assigning a single resource to a task

Here's how	**Here's why**
1 Switch to Gantt Chart view	Right-click the gray bar on the left side of the window and choose Gantt Chart.
2 Select task **8**	"Get approvals."
3 Click [Assign Resources icon]	(On the Resource tab.) To open the Assign Resources dialog box. You'll add resources to the task.
In the Resources from list, select **Pat Leary** and click **Assign**	(Scroll down to find the name.) To assign Pat Leary as a resource for this task.
4 Observe the Units field	(In the Assign Resources dialog box.) This field indicates that 100% of Pat Leary's time is assigned to this task.
5 Click **Close**	To close the dialog box.
6 Select task **9**	"Select architect."
7 Press (ALT) + (F10)	To open the Assign Resources dialog box.
In the Units field for Kathy Sinclair, type **20**	To assign Kathy to task 9, but using only 20% of her available time.
Click (TAB)	
8 Click **Close**	To close the Assign Resources dialog box.
9 Observe the Chart pane	
	(Scroll to the task, if necessary.) Assigned resource names appear to the right of their corresponding task bars.
10 Save your changes	

Multiple assignments

Explanation

You can assign a single resource to more than one task. For example, consider the tasks "Draw plans" and "Review blueprints." It makes sense that the architect would be assigned to both of these tasks.

To assign a single resource to multiple tasks:

1   Hold down Ctrl and select the tasks to which you want to assign a resource.
2   Open the Assign Resources dialog box. (You can also open the dialog box first and then select tasks in the Sheet pane.)
3   Select the resource name and click Assign.
4   Click Close.

Assigning multiple resources to a single task

You can also assign multiple resources to carry out a single task. To do so:

1   Open the Assign Resources dialog box.
2   Select the task to which you want to assign multiple resources. (Or select the task first and then open the Assign Resources dialog box.)
3   In the Assign Resources dialog box, select the first resource you want to assign.
4   Press and hold Ctrl, and select the other resources that you want to assign to the task.
5   Click Assign, and then click Close.

You can also select an individual resource, click Assign, select another resource and click Assign, and so on until you have completed your resource assignments.

Do it!

B-4:   Assigning multiple tasks and resources

Here's how	Here's why
1 Open the Assign Resources dialog box	Click the Assign Resources button or press Alt+F10.
Drag to select tasks 10 and 11	Both of these tasks ("Draw plans" and "Review blueprints") will be completed by the same resource, the architect.
2 Select **Architect**	In the Assign Resources dialog box.
Click **Assign**	To assign the resource to multiple tasks.
3 Select task 16	(Excavate for foundation.) Both Joe Simmons and the backhoe are needed to complete this task.
4 In the Assign Resources dialog box, select **Backhoe**	
Click **Assign**	
Select **Joe Simmons**	To select the second resource to be assigned to the task.
Click **Assign**	To assign multiple resources to a single task. Notice that Backhoe and Joe Simmons appear at the top of the list, with a checkmark next to each resource name.
5 Click **Close**	
6 Observe the task bar in the Chart pane	 (Scroll to the task, if necessary.) Both resources are displayed next to the task bar.
7 Save your changes	

Task calendars

Explanation

You might want to specify a working time that differs from the project calendar or the calendars of assigned resources. For example, resources might be available eight hours a day from Monday through Friday. However, the tools for the tasks might require maintenance every Friday. You can use the task calendar to define an exception for scheduling individual tasks that require equipment that runs during nonworking time or requires maintenance during working time.

By default, a calendar is not assigned to a task. Project schedules the task according to the working and nonworking times in the project calendar. However, when a task calendar or a resource calendar is assigned to a task, it takes precedence over the project calendar. If you have a task calendar and a calendar for the resource assigned to the task, you are prompted to specify which calendar will have precedence over the other.

Do it!

B-5:   Creating and applying a task calendar

Here's how	Here's why
1 Click the **Project** tab	
2 Open the Change Working Time dialog box	On the Ribbon, click Change Working Time.
Click **Create New Calendar**	
Type **Subcontracted tasks**	This will be the name of the new task calendar.
3 Verify that **Make a copy of** is selected	
Verify that **Outlander office construction** is selected	You'll create a copy of the current base calendar.
Click **OK**	
4 Observe the For calendar box	It displays the name of the base calendar you just created.
5 On the Exceptions tab, select the first Company holiday	March 9th, 2012, is highlighted in the calendar. You'll delete this holiday from the Subcontracted tasks calendar.
Click **Delete**	To remove the project holiday for non-employees.
Click **OK**	
6 Select task 16	(If necessary.) You'll apply the new calendar to this task.
Observe the start and finish dates	This task starts on 3/8/12 and finishes on 3/13/12, even though it's set to have a 3-day duration. This occurs because the company calendar is currently applied to the project, and in it, March 9th is designated as a company holiday.
7 Click the **Task** tab	
Click **Information**	(In the Properties group.) To open the Task Information dialog box.
Click the **Advanced** tab	

8	From the Calendar list, select **Subcontracted tasks**	You'll apply this calendar to the task.
	Check **Scheduling ignores resource calendars**	To specify that the task calendar takes precedence over the resource calendar.
	Click **OK**	To apply the Subcontracted tasks calendar to this task.
9	Click any cell to deselect task 16	
	Observe the Indicators field	An icon is displayed for this task because it uses a different calendar.
	Point to the icon	A ScreenTip appears, providing information about this task.
	Observe the new dates for the task	The task still begins on 3/8/12 but now ends on 3/12/12 because the Subcontracted tasks calendar is assigned to it, and this non-employee will work during the company holiday.
10	Save and close the project file	

Topic C: Project costs

Explanation

During the planning phase of your project, you can estimate resource costs. However, you need to estimate costs carefully to determine your project budget. Project helps you calculate resource costs at both the individual and overall levels of a project. You can enter resource costs in either Resource Sheet view or the Cost table.

Resource and task costs

You'll need to assign costs to each resource and task to determine the project budget. When you assign costs, Project calculates the overall cost of the project and the cost of individual tasks and resources. You might have different types of costs for different types of resources.

Cost types

Resource and task costs can be categorized as being fixed or variable. A *fixed cost* remains the same even if resources are added or taken away. For example, legal fees and permit fees are fixed costs.

A *variable cost* varies with the frequency and amount of time a resource is used. For example, a construction service company hires an excavator on an hourly basis. This cost varies depending on the number of hours the company needs the excavator.

There are three types of variable costs: standard costs, overtime costs, and per-use costs. They are described in the following table.

Variable cost	Description
Standard cost	The cost incurred to pay a resource for the hours the resource has worked on a task during the standard working hours as defined in a project.
Overtime cost	The cost incurred to pay a resource for the hours the resource has worked during overtime working hours as defined in a project.
Per-use cost	The cost incurred for the use of every unit of a resource in a task. Per-use cost is commonly used for resource materials, such as gravel, wood, and paint. Project multiplies the per-use cost by the number of units of the material used for the task to determine the total cost for the task and the resource.

C-1: Entering resource costs

The files for this activity are in Student Data folder **Unit 4\Topic C**.

Here's how	Here's why
1 Open New office Save the file as **My New office**	
2 In the status bar, click as shown	 To switch to Resource Sheet view. You'll assign costs to resources.
3 In the Std. Rate column, select the first cell	This cell contains the standard rate for the resource Kathy Sinclair.
Enter **62400/y**	Kathy is a salaried employee whose standard pay rate is $62,400 per year. Notice that when a field's entry is wider than the column, pounds signs are displayed.
4 Double-click where shown	 To expand the column width so that the values are visible. This method adjusts the column width to fit the widest cell in the column.
5 In the Std. Rate column, select the second cell	If necessary.
Enter **30**	The standard rate paid to David James is $30 per hour. The default unit is hours.
6 Set the standard rate for Pat Leary to **50,000/y**	In row 4.
7 Enter **25** as the standard rate for Contract laborers	In row 15.
8 Set the standard rate for Joe Simmons to **40**	
9 Verify that the standard rate for Architect is blank	You'll set a fixed cost for the architect's work in the next activity.
10 Set the remaining work resources to a standard rate of **20**	Do not change the rate for the architect and two cost resources.
11 Save your changes	

The Cost table

Explanation

Project provides predefined tables that you can apply to both tasks and resource views. The Cost table is one of them. The *Cost table* displays cost-related information about project tasks; this information includes fixed costs, baseline costs, variances, actual costs, and remaining costs. Exhibit 4-2 shows a Cost table in Task Sheet view.

To display the Cost table, click the View tab, click Tables, and choose Cost. The Total Cost field displays the cost for the task based on the standard rate of the resource. Project multiplies the value in the Std. Rate field for a resource by the number of days the resource is working on the task. For example, assume that the standard cost of a resource is $43.75 per hour. This resource is assigned to a task with a duration of four days. The total cost for this task is $1,400 ($43.75 multiplied by 8 hours, multiplied by 4 days).

	Task Name	Fixed	Fixed Cost	Total Cost	Baseline	Variance	Actual	Remaining
0	Constructing a new	$0.00	Prorated	$127,045.78	$0.00	$127,045.78	$0.00	$127,045.78
1	Review meeting	$0.00	Prorated	$840.38	$0.00	$840.38	$0.00	$840.38
7	Pre-construction	$0.00	Prorated	$74,069.23	$0.00	$74,069.23	$0.00	$74,069.23
8	Get approvals	$0.00	Prorated	$1,923.08	$0.00	$1,923.08	$0.00	$1,923.08
9	Select architect	$0.00	Prorated	$720.00	$0.00	$720.00	$0.00	$720.00
10	Draw plans	$60,000.00	Prorated	$67,200.00	$0.00	$67,200.00	$0.00	$67,200.00
11	Review blueprints	$0.00	Prorated	$2,880.00	$0.00	$2,880.00	$0.00	$2,880.00
12	Order materials	$0.00	Prorated	$1,346.15	$0.00	$1,346.15	$0.00	$1,346.15

Exhibit 4-2: A Cost table in Task Sheet view

Do it!   **C-2:**   **Using the Cost table**

Here's how	Here's why
1 Switch to Task Sheet view	Click the gray bar on the left side of the window and choose Task Sheet.
2 Click the **View** tab	If necessary.
3 Click **Tables** and choose **Cost**	To display the Cost table.
4 In row 9, observe the Total Cost field	The total cost for the task "Select architect" is $720. Kathy is assigned to this task, and she has a standard rate of $62,400 per year, or $1200 per week. This task has a duration of 3 weeks, and Kathy gives 20% of her time to this task, resulting in a total cost of $720.
5 In row 7, observe the Total Cost field	The total cost for this summary task is calculated automatically by adding the total costs of all of its subtasks.
6 Select the Fixed field for task 10	You'll enter a fixed cost for the task "Draw plans" because the architect will get a fixed amount for the project.
Enter **60000**	(Be sure to press Enter.) The fixed cost for this task is $60,000. The architect is paid by the job, not by the hour.
Observe the Total Cost field for the task Pre-construction	(In row 7.) The total cost for all subtasks has been updated.
7 Save and close the project file	

Unit summary: Resource management

Topic A   In this topic, you learned that a **base calendar** sets the working days and working hours for a project. You learned how to create a base calendar and change working time.

Topic B   In this topic, you learned how to create a **resource pool** by using Resource Sheet view. You learned how to create a resource calendar, assign resources to tasks, and create and apply a **task calendar**.

Topic C   In this topic, you learned how to record project **costs**. You learned how to enter resource costs in Resource Sheet view, and assign fixed costs by using the Cost table in Gantt Chart view.

Independent practice activity

In this activity, you'll create a base calendar, set a nonworking day, and assign the calendar as the project calendar. You'll also create a resource, set a nonworking day for the resource, and assign resources to tasks. Finally, you'll enter fixed costs for two tasks.

The files for this activity are in Student Data folder **Unit 4\Unit summary**.

1 Open Revised project.

2 Save the project file as **My Revised project**.

3 Open the Change Working Time dialog box.

4 Create a base calendar named **Office Project**.

5 Set Friday, April 22, 2011, as a nonworking day called **Holiday**.

6 Make Office Project the new project calendar. (*Hint:* Open the Project Information dialog box.)

7 Add a resource, **Laurie Macurthy**, to the Resource sheet. Assign her to Type, **Work**; Group, **Admin Assistant**; and Std. Rate, **$15.00/hr**.

8 Set February 14, 2011, as a personal vacation day for Laurie Macurthy. (*Hint:* Select Laurie Macurthy and click the Resource tab. Then click Information.)

9 Assign Laurie Macurthy to task 30.

10 Display the Cost table in Gantt Chart view. (*Hint:* Switch to Gantt Chart view, click the View tab, click Tables, and choose Cost.)

11 In the Fixed Cost field for task 26 (Get approvals), enter **300**.

12 For the task "Review blueprints", add a fixed cost of **4000**.

13 Save and close the project file.

Review questions

1 True or false? When you create a base calendar, it is automatically applied to the current project.

2 How do you open the Change Working Time dialog box?

3 What are two examples of a work resource?

4 What are two examples of a material resource?

5 What are two examples of a cost resource?

6 True or false? A resource calendar typically applies to all resources on a project.

7 What is the purpose of creating a task calendar?

8 What is a variable cost?

Unit 5

Views and tables

Unit time: 35 minutes

Complete this unit, and you'll know how to:

A Work in Calendar view and Resource Form view, add tasks to the Timeline, and format the Timeline.

B Work with tables, create a custom table, and display WBS outline numbers.

Topic A: Working with views

Explanation   Using different views allows you to focus on specific information. Project's many views enable you to enter, organize, and examine project information in a variety of ways. For example, to effectively monitor your project, you might want to look at all tasks ending in a specific week. You can do this in Calendar view. If you want to get information about a resource or a task, in isolation, you can use a form view. Generally, the views you use most often will be determined by personal preference, the nature of your project, and the specific information you want to focus on.

Calendar view

You can use *Calendar view* when you want to see project tasks that are scheduled for a specific day, week, or month in a calendar format. By default, Calendar view displays seven days and four weeks of the current month. (You can also display five days instead of all seven days in a week.) To navigate to other months, click the Previous and Next buttons or use the vertical scroll bar.

In Calendar view, each task is represented by a blue bar that spans days and weeks according to the task's schedule, as shown in Exhibit 5-1. Nonworking days are shaded in gray. The project summary task is displayed as a hollow task bar that acts as a header at the top of each week. Summary tasks for project phases are not displayed by default.

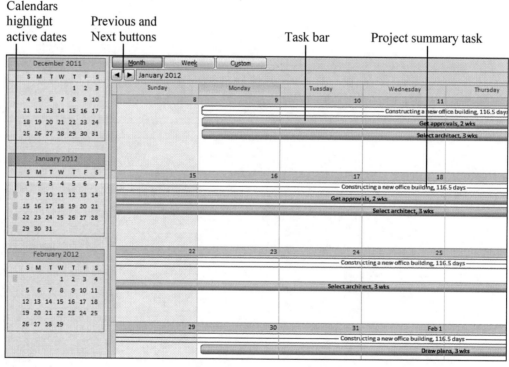

Exhibit 5-1: A sample Calendar view

Do it!

A-1:   **Exploring Calendar view**

The files for this activity are in Student Data folder **Unit 5\Topic A**.

Here's how	Here's why
1 Open New project	
Save the file as **My New project**	
2 Switch to Calendar view	(On the View tab, click Calendar. Or, right-click the gray bar and choose Calendar.) You'll explore this view.
3 Observe the window	The month and year of the project start date are displayed at the top. Blue task bars show task names and durations. Each week shows the project summary task at the top. The month calendars on the left side highlight the days that are displayed.
4 Locate the project completion milestone	(Use the vertical scroll bar.) In Calendar view, milestone tasks appear as black bars.
5 Point to the top of a date bar, as shown	
	The pointer changes so you can grab the calendar row.
Drag down about 1/2"	To increase the height of the calendar row. In a complex and packed schedule, some task bars might be hidden, so you'll need to increase the height of the rows.
6 Double-click the top of any date bar, as shown	
	To adjust the height of all calendar rows uniformly to show all task bars.
7 Save your changes	

Form views

Form views provide detailed information about an individual task or resource. For example, if you want to view schedule or cost-related information for Kathy Sinclair, you can use Resource Form view, which shows complete information pertaining only to Kathy Sinclair.

The following table describes the form views.

Form view	Description
Resource Form	Provides detailed information for a single resource. Click the Previous and Next buttons to view information on previous or subsequent resources.
Resource Name Form	A simplified version of Resource Form view. You can use this view to see all tasks assigned to a resource.
Task Details Form	Provides details on a single task. Click the Previous and Next buttons to view information on previous or subsequent tasks.
Task Form	Similar to the Task Details Form, but excludes some information, such as constraints, priority, and the task's WBS code.
Task Name Form	Another simplified version of the Task Details Form. Use this view for assigned resource and predecessor information only.

To switch to a form view, right-click the gray bar on the left side of the window and choose the desired view. If the form you're looking for is not in the menu, choose More Views. Then scroll to locate and select the desired form, and click Apply.

Each form provides buttons on the Format tab that allow you to quickly switch between the different versions of the form. For example, in Task Form view, you can click the Task Details Form button or the Task Name Form button to toggle between form variations.

Split views

With a split view, you can work in a task view, such as Gantt Chart view, while viewing related resource information in an easy-to-read form. For example, if you want to review your task list and see information such as a task's assigned resources and their total hours assigned to the task, switch to Gantt Chart view and click the View tab. Then, in the Split View group, check Details. This action splits the window into two panes, with the Gantt Chart at the top and the Task Form at the bottom. You can then switch the bottom pane to any other view by selecting an option from the Details list.

You can't show the Timeline in a split view. If the Details option is checked, checking Timeline will clear the Details option, and vice versa.

You can also split a view by clicking the Resource tab and then clicking Details. This shows the Resource Form below the current view.

Do it!

A-2: Applying Form views

Here's how	Here's why
1 Switch to Resource Form view	(Right-click the gray bar and choose Resource Form. Or, in the Resource Views group, select Other views, Resource Form.) Information about Kathy Sinclair is displayed because she's the first resource listed in the Resource Sheet.
Observe the Task Name column	This column displays all tasks to which Kathy Sinclair is assigned.
2 Click **Next**	To see information about the next person in the resource list, David James.
Observe the other columns	You can quickly view the tasks, schedule, and pay rates associated with an individual resource.
3 Click the **Format** tab	
Click **Work** and observe the columns	With this option selected, you can view all work-related information, including the work units and the hours of work remaining for each task.
4 Click **Resource Name Form**	This view of the form provides fewer details.
Click **Resource Form**	To return to the more detailed form.
5 Click **Cost**	To change the field headings again, this time to show cost information for the resource.
6 Switch to Gantt Chart view	
7 Click the **View** tab	If necessary.
In the Split View group, check **Details**	The window is split, with Gantt Chart view at the top and Task Form view at the bottom. Notice that the Timeline is no longer visible.
8 From the list next to Details, select **Resource Form**	
9 In the task list, select **Order materials**	(Task 12.) You'll edit resource cost information.
In the Resource Form, change the overtime rate to **25/h**	
Click **OK**	To apply the resource cost change.

Working with the Timeline

Explanation

Timeline view provides a graphical, high-level view of your project, which you can customize in several ways and share with other Office applications such as Outlook. Gantt with Timeline view, the default view in Project 2010, shows the Timeline above the Sheet and Chart panes. Timeline view displays only the project timeline.

The Timeline at the top of Gantt with Timeline view provides an easy way to navigate project tasks and focus on specific dates. You can also add tasks to the Timeline to create a "big picture" view of your project, which you can format and use for project presentations and reviews with stakeholders.

To add tasks to the Timeline, first select a range of tasks. Then right-click the selection and choose Add to Timeline. By default, the tasks appear as blue rectangles, sized according to their duration.

Timeline formatting

After you have added tasks to the Timeline, you can format the Timeline in many ways. For example, you can apply different colors and fonts, use callouts for task names, and change the date format, as shown in Exhibit 5-2.

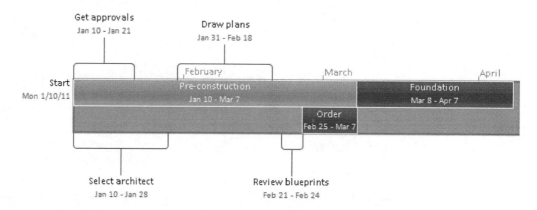

Exhibit 5-2: An example of Timeline formatting

Do it!

A-3:   **Working with the Timeline**

Here's how	Here's why
1 On the View tab, in the Split View group, check **Timeline**	To return to Gantt Chart view with the Timeline at the top.
Observe the Timeline	It displays the project start and finish dates.
2 In the Timeline, point as shown	
	The pointer changes to a two-headed arrow, indicating that you can drag in either direction.
Drag to the right	As you drag, more of the task bars come into view because you are focusing on a longer time range.
3 In the Sheet pane, right-click the project summary task	
Choose **Add to Timeline**	The project summary task is now displayed on the Timeline.
4 Point to the border below the Timeline, as shown	
Drag to about halfway down the window	To increase the size of the Timeline.
5 Drag to select tasks 7–13	In the Sheet pane.
Add the selected tasks to the Timeline	Right-click the selection and choose Add to Timeline.
6 Drag **Get approvals** above the Timeline, as shown	
	To format the subtask as a callout.
7 Drag **Select architect** below the Timeline	To format the subtask as a callout.

8	In the Timeline, click **Pre-construction**	To select it.
	Click the **Format** tab	If necessary.
	Click as shown
To open a color palette.
	Select the orange color in the first row of the palette	
9	Click **Date Format**	In the Show/Hide group.
	Choose **Jan 28**	To apply a concise date format to the Timeline.
10	Make the task "Draw plans" a callout below the Timeline	
11	Make "Review blueprints" a callout above the Timeline	
12	Point as shown	
	Drag to the right	To view more of the Timeline. The area outside the edge appears dimmed to indicate that it's not in focus in the Chart pane.
13	Switch to Timeline view	(Right-click the gray bar and choose Timeline. Or, select Timeline from the More Views dialog box.) To see the Timeline in a full screen.
14	Save your changes	

Sharing project information with external stakeholders

Explanation

With Project 2010's enhanced copy and paste feature, you can copy the Timeline into other Office applications. On the Format tab, click Copy Timeline and then select For E-mail, For Presentation, or Full Size. For example, you can paste a Timeline into PowerPoint 2010 as a collection of individual Office Art objects; you can then apply additional formatting to each component of the Timeline by using PowerPoint's formatting tools. You can select For E-mail and paste the Timeline into an Outlook message to share project details with stakeholders.

Do it! **A-4:   Copying a Timeline into PowerPoint**

Here's how	Here's why
1 Click the **Format** tab	
2 Click **Copy Timeline**	
Choose **For Presentation**	
3 Click **Start** and choose **All Programs, Microsoft Office, Microsoft PowerPoint 2010**	To open PowerPoint. A blank default slide is displayed.
4 Click **New Slide** and choose **Blank**	To start with a blank slide.
5 Click **Paste**	The Timeline appears on the slide.
Click an empty area in the Timeline	To select it
6 Point to the bottom edge, as shown	
Drag down	To increase the size of the Timeline.
7 Double-click the project summary task	(Constructing a new office building.) You'll format this as an individual Office Art object.
8 Click **Shape Effects** and choose **Preset**	
Under Presets, click the second option	To apply an outer bevel to the summary task. This is just an example of how you can format each object in the Timeline separately.
9 Close PowerPoint	
Click **Don't Save**	
10 Save and close the project file	

Topic B: Working with tables

Explanation

Tables are variations of the default Sheet pane layout. You can use tables to focus your project data to show specific information about tasks and resources. Many tables share common information, such as the Task Name and Duration columns. The default Sheet pane layout is called the Entry table. Other built-in tables include the Cost table, the Work table, and the Usage table.

You can customize tables to meet your needs. For example, you can modify the Cost table to show only the columns of information that you want, or adjust column widths and alignment to suit your preferences.

Custom tables

To create a custom table, click the View tab, click Tables, and choose More Tables. This opens the More Tables dialog box. You can then create a table by clicking the New button, naming the table, and selecting the desired columns. Or, to save time selecting columns, you can create a table based on an existing table and then change it to suit your needs.

To create a table based on an existing table:

1   On the View tab, click Tables and choose More Tables.
2   Select the table that you want to base the new table on.
3   Click Copy to open the Table Definition dialog box.
4   In the Name box, type a name for the table.
5   In the list of fields, modify the field name, alignment, width, title, or title alignment as needed
6   Click OK, and then click Apply to apply the new table to the Sheet pane.

You can insert, delete, cut, or copy rows to modify your table fields. To insert a new field into a table:

1   In the Table Definition dialog box, select the field above which you want to insert a row.
2   Click Insert Row.
3   From the field name list, select the desired field name.
4   Click OK.
5   Click Apply.

Displaying WBS outline numbers

The WBS (Work Breakdown Structure) depicts the hierarchy of tasks in your project as an outline. Each task has a unique outline number that indicates its level in the task hierarchy. For example, in Exhibit 5-3, "Review meeting" and "Pre-construction" are the main tasks under the project summary task. Therefore, they have the WBS codes 1 and 2, respectively. "Get approvals" and "Select architect" are subtasks of the summary task "Pre-construction." Therefore, they have the WBS codes 2.1 and 2.2, respectively.

By default, the Sheet pane does not include a WBS column. To show the WBS column, you need to add it to the Sheet pane or include it in a table you create.

To insert the WBS column:

1   Right-click the column heading that's to the right of where you want to insert the WBS column.

2   Choose Insert Column.

3   Type WBS and press Enter.

4   Resize the column as needed.

You can also add a WBS column to a table by using the Table Definition dialog box.

WBS code field

	WBS	ⓘ	Task Name	Duration	Start	Finish
0	0		⊟ Constructing a new	103.5 days	Mon 1/28/08	Tue 6/24/08
1	1	↻	⊞ Review meeting	87.25 days	Fri 2/1/08	Fri 6/6/08
7	2		⊟ Pre-construction	41 days	Mon 1/28/08	Wed 3/26/08
8	2.1		Get approvals	2 wks	Mon 1/28/08	Fri 2/8/08
9	2.2		Select architect	3 wks	Mon 1/28/08	Fri 2/15/08
10	2.3		Draw plans	3 wks	Tue 2/19/08	Mon 3/10/08
11	2.4		Review blueprints	4 days	Tue 3/11/08	Fri 3/14/08
12	2.5		Order materials	7 days	Tue 3/18/08	Wed 3/26/08
13	3		⊟ Foundation	11 days	Thu 3/27/08	Fri 4/11/08
14	3.1	📋	Excavate for found	3 days	Thu 3/27/08	Mon 3/31/08
15	3.2		Install drainage	3 days	Tue 4/1/08	Thu 4/3/08
16	3.3		Lay slab foundatior	2 days	Fri 4/4/08	Mon 4/7/08
17	3.4		Install external utiliti	4 days	Tue 4/8/08	Fri 4/11/08

Exhibit 5-3: WBS codes

Displaying the WBS in the Task Name field

If you want to see the WBS but you prefer not to create a separate column for the outline numbers, you can display the numbers directly in the Task Name field, right before each task name. To do so, click the Format tab and check Outline Number.

Replacing columns

You can replace any column with a new column. To do so, double-click the column heading to display a list of available columns. Select the column name from the list to replace the previous column.

Do it!

B-1:   Creating a table and displaying WBS codes

The files for this activity are in Student Data folder **Unit 5\Topic B**.

Here's how	Here's why
1 Open New project 2	
Save the file as **My New project 2**	
2 Switch to Task Sheet view	
Click the **View** tab	If necessary.
3 Click **Tables** and choose **More Tables...**	To open the More Tables dialog box.
From the Tables list, select **Entry**	
Click **Copy**	To open the Table Definition dialog box. You will copy the information in the Entry table.
4 In the Name box, enter **Entry with WBS**	To name the table according to what it will display.
5 In the Field Name field, select **Indicators**	You'll insert a row above this field.
Click **Insert Row**	To insert a field between ID and Indicators in the new table.
6 Click the arrow to open the new row list	
Type **W**	To go directly to the options beginning with "W."
Select **WBS**	
Click **OK**	Notice that "Entry with WBS" is selected in the More Tables dialog box.
7 Click **Apply**	To view the new table. A new field showing WBS codes is displayed.
Double-click the right edge of the WBS column heading	To make the column only as wide as the widest cell in the column.
8 Click the **WBS** column heading	To select the column.
Press (*DELETE*)	To remove the column from the table.

9 Click the **Format** tab

   Check **Outline Number**   To display the WBS outline numbers before the task names.

10 Double-click the **Predecessors** column heading   You'll replace this column.

   Type **c**   To jump to options beginning with the letter "c."

   Select **Cost**   To add this field to the table.

11 Save and close the project file

Unit summary: Views and tables

Topic A   In this topic, you learned how to work in **Calendar view** and **Resource Form view**. You learned that form views provide detailed information about an individual task or resource. You learned how to add tasks to the **Timeline** to create a "big picture" view of your project. You also learned how to format the Timeline for project presentations and for sharing with stakeholders via other Office 2010 applications, such as Outlook and PowerPoint.

Topic B   In this topic, you learned how to work with **tables** and create tables. You also learned how to display **WBS outline numbers** in a separate column and directly in the Task Name column.

Independent practice activity

In this activity, you'll switch to Resource Name Form view and change the detail view to find cost information for a specific resource. Then, you'll create a task table based on another table and modify the table information displayed.

The files for this activity are in Student Data folder **Unit 5\Unit summary**.

1 Open New construction project.

2 Save the file as **My New construction project**.

3 Add tasks 7–13 to the Timeline.

4 Apply a different color to the summary task and the milestone task in the Timeline.

5 Switch to Resource Name Form view. (*Hint:* Click the View button and choose More Views.)

6 Navigate to view Ann Salinski's information.

7 Change the detail view to get information on her schedule. (*Hint:* Click the Format tab.)

8 Switch to Task Sheet view.

9 Create a new task table based on the table **Schedule**, and name it **Track schedule**. Insert a row for **%Complete**. Set the Width of this field to **12**. (*Hint:* First, click the View tab, click Tables, and choose More Tables.)

10 View the new table. Resize the columns to show all the content.

11 Insert a new column next to the Start column. Choose the Field name **Type**.

12 Hide the Late Start and Late Finish columns.

13 Save and close the project file.

Review questions

1 By default, Calendar view displays seven days and four weeks of the current month. How do you navigate to other months?

2 What are some advantages of using the Timeline?

3 How can you add WBS outline numbers directly in the Task Name field?

4 Why might you want to create a custom table?

5 True or false? The default Sheet pane layout is one of many tables.

Unit 6

Filters, groups, and sorting

Unit time: 60 minutes

Complete this unit, and you'll know how to:

A Apply filters, highlighting, and AutoFilters, and create custom filters.

B Group tasks and resources, and create custom groups.

C Sort tasks and resources, and renumber a sorted task or resource list.

Topic A: Filters

Explanation

At times, you'll likely need to concentrate on a specific set of tasks or resources. For example, you might need to see the costs for only certain resources or review only critical tasks. You can do this by filtering a view.

Applying filters

Project provides several built-in filters, which you can apply by using the Filter list on the View tab. If you're using a task-related view, the options in the Filter list pertain to tasks. If you're using a resource-related view, the options pertain to resources and costs. When you filter a view, no information is deleted; it's simply hidden to allow you to focus on the selected information.

To filter a view:

1 Click the View tab.
2 From the Filter list, select a filter.
3 To return to an unfiltered view, select [No Filter] from the Filter list.

Highlighting information

Like filters, highlighting helps you to focus on a subset of information in a view. Unlike filters, highlighting does not hide any information; it just changes the text color of the information you want to highlight. To highlight information in a view, select an option from the Highlight list on the View tab.

Do it!

A-1:   Filtering and highlighting information

The files for this activity are in Student Data folder **Unit 6\Topic A**.

Here's how	Here's why
1 Open Outlander office	
Save the project file as **My Outlander office**	You'll filter tasks by using a standard filter.
2 Observe the task list	The complete task list is visible; no filters are applied to this view.
3 Click the **View** tab	
4 Click as shown	To display the Filter list.
Observe the filter options	You can filter a view to focus on active tasks, completed tasks, critical tasks, tasks in a specified date range, and so on.

5 From the Filter list, select **Summary Tasks**	To view only the summary tasks. Notice that the summary tasks cannot be expanded in the Sheet pane, and only summary task bars are displayed in the Chart pane.
6 Open the Filter list	
Select **[No Filter]**	To return to an unfiltered view.
7 From the Filter list, select **Using Resource...**	To open the Using Resource dialog box.
From the "Show tasks using" list, select **David James**	
Click **OK**	To show only those tasks assigned to David James. "David James" is displayed in the Resource Names column for each activity.
8 In the Task Name field, select **External work**	
Press CTRL + SHIFT + F5	To scroll to the selected task in the Chart pane. All of the task bars show that David James is assigned to each task.
9 Switch to Resource Sheet view	
Open the Filter list	In this view, all of the filters pertain to resources and costs, rather than to tasks.
Select **Resources–Material**	To show only material resources.
10 Unfilter the view	Next, you'll highlight information.
11 From the Highlight list, select **Resources-Work**	Working resources are highlighted in blue, while material resources remain black. Highlighting does not hide any information from a view; it allows you to focus on specific information by changing the text color.
12 Save your changes	

AutoFilters

Explanation

AutoFilters are another tool you can use to focus on specific information. You apply an AutoFilter to a view by clicking the arrow on the right edge of any column. This opens a list of commands, including a list of all items in that column. You can uncheck the items that you don't want to view and click OK, or you can click Filters and select a built-in AutoFilter.

You might want to first apply a standard filter and then use a column's AutoFilter to fine-tune that filtered view. For example, after applying the Date Range filter to display only tasks in a specified date range, you might want to then show only those tasks in that subset that will take one week or longer to complete. To do this, you would apply an AutoFilter to the Duration field.

To apply an AutoFilter:

1   In the Sheet pane, click the arrow on the right edge of the column you want to filter by.

2   Do either of the following:

- Click Filters and select a built-in filter.
- Clear Select All, and then check only those items that you want to show.

When a filter is applied to a column, the arrow in the column heading is replaced by a funnel icon. To turn off that filter, click the funnel icon and select "Clear Filter from (*Column Name*)."

Do it!

A-2:   Applying AutoFilters

Here's how	Here's why
1 Switch to Gantt Chart view	
2 Click the arrow in the Duration column heading	A list of commands is displayed.
3 Click **Filters** and select **1 week or longer**	The task list now shows only those tasks with a duration of one week or more.
Observe the Duration column heading	Duration ⧩ The funnel icon indicates that the current view is filtered by a duration variable.
4 From the Filter list on the View tab, select **Using Resource...**	You'll apply a standard filter to this already filtered view.
From the "Show tasks using" list, select **Ann Salinski**	To show only those tasks assigned to Ann Salinski that have a duration of one week or more.
5 From the Filter list on the View tab, select **[No Filter]**	This action also clears the AutoFilter that was applied to the Duration column.

6 Click the arrow in the Duration column heading	You'll apply a different AutoFilter.
Clear **(Select All)**	(Click it.) To clear the default selections.
Check **6 days** and click **OK**	To show only those tasks with a duration of 6 days, plus the summary tasks with which they are associated.
7 Click the arrow in the Resource Names column heading	
Clear **(Select All)**	
Check **Curt Allen** and click **OK**	To show only those tasks assigned to Curt Allen that have a duration of exactly 6 days. (One less task is displayed.)
8 Observe the Duration and Resource Names headings	Both column headings have a funnel icon; the current view is filtered by criteria in both columns.
9 Unfilter the list	From the Filter list on the View tab, select No Filter.
10 Save your changes	

Custom filters

Explanation

You can create your own custom filters to selectively show a task or resource list. When you apply a custom filter, a dialog box opens in which you can enter your filter criteria. For example, to filter tasks or resources for a specific cost value, switch to the Cost table within the respective view. Then create your filter.

To create a custom filter:

1 On the View tab, from the Filter list, select More Filters to open the More Filters dialog box.

2 Click New to open the Filter Definition dialog box.

3 In the Name box, type a name for the filter.

4 Verify that "Show in menu" is checked so that the new filter will appear in the full list of filters.

5 Under Field Name, select the first cell to display its drop-down arrow. Click the arrow to open the list and select a field name.

6 Under Test, select a test from the list.

7 In the Value(s) field, type a message in quotation marks, followed by a question mark.

8 Click OK to close the Filter Definition dialog box.

9 Click Apply to use the filter now, or click Cancel to use the filter later.

Custom filters don't carry over to a different view. After you apply a filter to a view and switch to another view, the unfiltered list is displayed.

Do it!

A-3: Creating a custom filter

Here's how	Here's why
1 Switch to Resource Sheet view	
2 On the View tab, click **Tables** and choose **Cost**	To switch to the Cost table and view cost-related information. A Baseline Cost has not been entered; therefore, the Cost, Variance, and Remaining fields all contain the same values.
3 From the Filter list, select **More Filters...**	To open the More Filters dialog box.
4 Click **New...**	To open the Filter Definition dialog box. You'll create a custom filter.
5 In the Name box, type **Resource cost**	This will be the name of your filter.
Verify that **Show in menu** is checked	To add this filter to the list of filters.
6 Under Field Name, select the first cell	To display its drop-down list.
From the Field Name list, select **Cost**	To filter the task list based on cost.

7 Under Test, select the first cell

   From the Test list, select | This is the criterion by which you'll filter the
   is greater than | project information.

8 In the Value(s) field, type | This will be the message in the dialog box. The
   "Cost greater than"? | question mark tells Project to open a custom
   | dialog box when the filter is applied.

9 Click **Save** | To return to the More Filters dialog box.

   Select **Resource cost** | This is the filter you just created.

   Click **Apply**

10 Observe the dialog box

Project displays a custom dialog box called
Resource cost and displays the message you
entered—Cost greater than.

   Type **4000** and click **OK** | To filter the list based on the specified value.
   | Only four resources have a cost of over $4000.

11 Observe the Filter list box

Resource cost is the active filter.

   Run the filter again | From the Filter list, select Resource cost.

   Type **2000** and click **OK** | To show all resources whose cost is greater than
   | $2000.

12 From the Filter list, select | To show the entire list of resources again.
   [No Filter]

13 Save and close the project file

Topic B: Groups

Explanation

You can group tasks or resources in a view to organize project information without changing the actual structure of the project. Grouping items can help you to refine your project or work out a scheduling problem. For example, you might want to group tasks based on their duration to identify the longest and shortest tasks.

Grouping tasks and resources

The grouping options that are available depend on the view you're working in. You can apply task-related groups to task-related views, such as the Gantt Chart, Task Usage, and Tracking Gantt views. You can apply resource-related groups to resource views, such as the Resource Sheet, Resource Usage, and Resource Allocation views. You cannot group information in the Calendar, Network Diagram, or Resources Graph views.

To group items in a task list or resource list, click the View tab and select an option from the Group by list. The results appear in the Sheet pane, with information grouped by the specified criterion. As shown in Exhibit 6-1, highlighting helps to visually separate each group, and headings for each group are automatically created based on the group's criterion.

		Task Name	Duration	Start	Finish	Resource Names
		⊟ **Duration: 2 days**	**2d**	**Tue 3/8/11**	**Wed 6/22/11**	
32		Survey and stake	2 days	Tue 3/8/11	Wed 3/9/11	
38		Lay slab foundation	2 days	Mon 4/4/11	Tue 4/5/11	Joe Simmons
39		Backfill	2 days	Wed 4/6/11	Thu 4/7/11	
52		Insulation	2 days	Mon 5/16/11	Tue 5/17/11	
54		Paint	2 days	Tue 5/24/11	Wed 5/25/11	David James,Ann Salinski,Curt Allen
55		Install flooring	2 days	Fri 5/27/11	Mon 5/30/11	David James,Ann Salinski,Jerry Davis
59		Certificate of Occupancy	2 days	Mon 6/20/11	Wed 6/22/11	Kathy Sinclair[25%],Pat Leary[25%]
		⊟ **Duration: 3 days**	**3d**	**Thu 3/10/11**	**Fri 5/6/11**	
33		Excavate for foundation	3 days	Thu 3/10/11	Mon 3/14/11	Backhoe,Joe Simmons
34		Footings	3 days	Tue 3/15/11	Thu 3/17/11	
35		Install drainage	3 days	Fri 3/18/11	Tue 3/22/11	Joe Simmons
44		Install siding	3 days	Thu 4/28/11	Mon 5/2/11	Ann Salinski,Curt Allen,Jerry Davis
51		Distribute water, sewer	3 days	Wed 5/4/11	Fri 5/6/11	Laurie Macurthy,Tim Walson,Peter Jones[50%]
		⊟ **Duration: 4 days**	**4d**	**Mon 2/21/11**	**Mon 6/20/11**	
28		Review blueprints	4 days	Mon 2/21/11	Thu 2/24/11	Architect,Kathy Sinclair
36		Install external utilities	4 days	Wed 3/23/11	Mon 3/28/11	Peter Jones,Susan Gianni,Fred Little,Ann Salinski,Curt Allen
37		Foundation walls	4 days	Tue 3/29/11	Fri 4/1/11	
41		Erect steel frame	4 days	Fri 4/8/11	Wed 4/13/11	David James,Jerry Davis,Laurie Macurthy
43		Install windows, external doors	4 days	Fri 4/22/11	Wed 4/27/11	David James,Laurie Macurthy,Tim Walson,Contract laborers[20
45		Install roof	4 days	Fri 4/22/11	Wed 4/27/11	Ann Salinski,Curt Allen,Jerry Davis,Contract laborers[200%]
47		Frame internal walls	4 days	Thu 4/28/11	Tue 5/3/11	David James,Laurie Macurthy,Tim Walson
53		Install & finish drywall	4 days	Wed 5/18/11	Mon 5/23/11	David James,Laurie Macurthy,Tim Walson
58		Install furnishings	4 days	Tue 6/14/11	Mon 6/20/11	Laurie Macurthy,Tim Walson,David James

Exhibit 6-1: A grouped task list

You can also apply groups by clicking the drop-down arrow in the Group By box on the View tab and selecting a group from the list.

Do it!

B-1:   Grouping tasks

The files for this activity are in Student Data folder **Unit 6\Topic B**.

Here's how	Here's why
1 Open Outlander office 2	
Save the project file as **My Outlander office 2**	You'll arrange tasks by using a predefined group.
2 Click the **View** tab	
From the Group by list, select **Duration**	To group the tasks based on their duration. The tasks with the shortest duration are displayed first. The highlighting helps you distinguish the groups.
3 From the Group by list, select **Resource**	

4 Click as shown	Task Name
	
	⊟ Resource Names: No Value
	     Weekly status 1
	     Weekly status 2
	
	To hide the weekly status meetings and show more resource groups.

5 From the Group by list, select **[No Group]**	To show the task list without grouping.
6 Save your changes	

Custom groups

Explanation

If the predefined groups do not return the information you need, you can create a custom group to selectively group tasks and resources.

To create a custom group:

1 On the View tab, from the Group by list, select More Groups.
2 Click New to open the Group Definition dialog box.
3 In the Name box, type a name for the group.
4 Under Field Name, select the first cell and then select a field name from the list.
5 Under Order, select the first cell and then select an option from the list.
6 Click Define Group Intervals. From the Group on list, select an option. Click OK.
7 Click Save to return to the More Groups dialog box.
8 Click Apply to group the information.

Editing and copying a group

You can also customize and reuse a group definition by editing or copying a group. To do so:

1 On the View tab, from the Group by list, select More Groups.
2 Click Edit (or Copy, if you want to copy the group) to open the Group Definition dialog box.
3 Modify the fields to suit your requirements.
4 Click Save to close the Group Definition dialog box.
5 Click Apply to group the information.

Do it!

B-2:   Creating a custom group

Here's how	Here's why
1 From the Group by list, select **More Groups...**	(On the View tab.) To open the More Groups dialog box.
2 Click **New...**	To open the Group Definition dialog box. You'll create a custom group.
In the Name box, type **Duration in weeks**	This will be the name of the group.
3 Click under Field Name	To display a drop-down arrow.
From the Field Name list, select **Duration**	(Scroll down or begin typing to jump to Duration in the list.) To group the tasks based on their duration.
4 Under Order, click **Ascending**	(This is the default sort order.) A drop-down arrow is displayed.
From the Order list, select **Descending**	You'll group the tasks by duration in descending order.
5 Click **Define Group Intervals...**	(On the lower left side of the dialog box.) To open the Define Group Interval dialog box.
From the Group on list, select **Weeks**, and click **OK**	To group the tasks based on duration in weeks.
6 Click **Save**	To return to the More Groups dialog box.
7 In the Groups list, verify that **Duration in weeks** is selected	
Click **Apply**	To apply the custom group. All tasks are grouped based on their duration in weeks in descending order.
8 From the Group by list, select **No Group**	To show the tasks without grouping.
9 Save and close the project file	

Topic C: Sorting tasks and resources

Explanation
Sorting displays tasks or resources in a specified sequence. You can sort tasks by criteria including cost, start date, and finish date.

Sorting tasks

When you sort tasks, the task ID numbers do not change, so the task IDs will often appear out of sequence. You can restore the task list to its default order by sorting the tasks by ID. To sort a task list, click the View tab, click Sort, and select a sort option.

Do it!
C-1: Sorting a task list

The files for this activity are in Student Data folder **Unit 6\Topic C**.

Here's how	Here's why
1 Open Current project	
Save the file as **My Current project**	
2 Observe tasks 49, 50, and 51	(Scroll down if necessary.) These three tasks start on the same date but finish on different dates. You'll sort the task list by finish dates.
3 On the View tab, click **Sort**	
Select **by Finish Date**	To sort tasks by their finish date in ascending order.
4 Observe the task list	Tasks 49 through 51 are now in a different order based on their finish dates.
Observe the task IDs	Because task 51 finishes before tasks 49 and 50, it's listed first.
5 Click **Sort** and select **by ID**	To return the tasks to their original order.

Sorting resources

Explanation

You can sort resources to view them in a desired sequence. For example, you might want to view all resources in alphabetical order. To sort a resource list, switch to Resource Sheet view. On the View tab, click Sort to open a list of options. You can sort resources based on criteria including group, name, and cost.

You can apply more than one sort criterion. For example, you can sort resources alphabetically by group, and then sort the grouped resources by their names.

As with tasks, when you sort a resource list, the resource ID numbers do not change, so the IDs might appear out of sequence, as shown in Exhibit 6-2. To restore the resource list to its default order, sort the resources by ID.

	ⓘ	Resource Name ▼	Type ▼	Material ▼	Initials ▼	Group ▼
3		Pat Leary	Work		PL	Admin. Assist
14		Contract laborers	Work		C	Contract labor
10		Architect	Work		A	External
8		Joe Simmons	Work		JS	External
15		Backhoe	Work		b	Hired equipme
6		Ann Salinski	Work		AS	Labor
4		Curt Allen	Work		CA	Labor
2	◈	David James	Work		DJ	Labor
12		Jerry Davis	Work		JD	Labor
13		Laurie Macurthy	Work		LM	Labor
11		Tim Walson	Work		TW	Labor
1		Kathy Sinclair	Work		KS	Project mgmt.
17		Metal stud	Material	each	ms	Purchased
16		Paint	Material	gallon	p	Purchased
9		Fred Little	Work		FL	Skilled labor
5		Peter Jones	Work		PJ	Skilled labor
7		Susan Gianni	Work		SG	Skilled labor

Exhibit 6-2: A sorted resource sheet

Do it!   **C-2:**   **Sorting a resource list**

Here's how	Here's why
1 Switch to Resource Sheet view	You'll sort resources based on specific criteria.
2 Click **Sort** and choose **Sort By…**	To open the Sort dialog box. You'll sort resources by more than one criterion.
Verify that "Permanently renumber resources" is cleared	This option is cleared by default so that you can arrange the resources by their original IDs after sorting.
3 From the Sort by list, select **Group**	This will be the first criterion for sorting the resources.
4 From the Then by list, select **Name**	This will be the second criterion.
5 Click **Sort**	To sort the resource names first by Group and then by Name.
6 Save your changes	

Renumbering a sorted list

Explanation   Sorting does not change the ID numbers of tasks or resources, and the resulting non-sequential ID numbers might not suit your needs or preferences. You can renumber sorted tasks and resources in their respective sheets. When you do, the original order of each sheet is changed. Exhibit 6-3 shows the same resource list as Exhibit 6-2, but with new resource ID numbers.

To renumber resources or tasks:

1 On the View tab, click Sort and choose Sort by.
2 Check "Permanently renumber resources" (or "Permanently renumber tasks," depending on the view).
3 Click Sort.

	❶	Resource Name ▼	Type ▼	Material ▼	Initial ▼	Group ▼
1		Pat Leary	Work		PL	Admin. Assist
2		Contract laborers	Work		C	Contract labor
3		Architect	Work		A	External
4		Joe Simmons	Work		JS	External
5		Backhoe	Work		b	Hired equipme
6		Ann Salinski	Work		AS	Labor
7		Curt Allen	Work		CA	Labor
8	◇	David James	Work		DJ	Labor
9		Jerry Davis	Work		JD	Labor
10		Laurie Macurthy	Work		LM	Labor
11		Tim Walson	Work		TW	Labor
12		Kathy Sinclair	Work		KS	Project mgmt.
13		Metal stud	Material	each	ms	Purchased
14		Paint	Material	gallon	p	Purchased
15		Fred Little	Work		FL	Skilled labor
16		Peter Jones	Work		PJ	Skilled labor
17		Susan Gianni	Work		SG	Skilled labor

Exhibit 6-3: The sorted resource list renumbered

Do it!   **C-3:   Renumbering a sorted resource list**

Here's how	Here's why
1 Click **Sort** and choose **Sort By…**	To open the Sort dialog box You'll renumber the sorted resource list.
2 Check **Permanently renumber resources**	If you're in a resource view, the Sort dialog box shows a "Permanently renumber resources" option. When you're in a task view, it shows a "Permanently renumber tasks" option.
Click **Sort**	To establish a new order for the resources.
3 Observe the ID field	The sorted resources have new ID numbers.
4 Save and close the project file	

Unit summary: Filters, groups, and sorting

Topic A   In this topic, you learned how to apply **filters** so that you can focus on a specific set of tasks or resources and hide information you don't need to see. You learned how to **highlight** certain information, use AutoFilters, and create your own custom filters to selectively view a task or resource list.

Topic B   In this topic, you learned how to **group tasks and resources** to organize project information without changing the structure of the project. You also learned how to create custom groups to selectively arrange tasks and resources.

Topic C   In this topic, you learned how to **sort tasks** and **resources** to display project information in a desired sequence. Finally, you learned how to permanently renumber a sorted task or resource list.

Independent practice activity

In this activity, you'll apply filters to view specific information. Then you'll filter a view by group and sort resources by multiple criteria.

The files for this activity are in Student Data folder **Unit 6\Unit summary**.

1 Open Construction.

2 Save the file as **My Construction**.

3 Filter the task list to show only those tasks to which Tim Walson is assigned. (*Hint:* Apply the Using Resource filter.)

4 Apply an AutoFilter to show only those tasks with a duration of 1 week or more.

5 Unfilter the task list. (*Hint:* Use the Filter list.)

6 Switch to Resource Sheet view. Use the Group column's AutoFilter to show only those resources that belong to the group Skilled labor. (*Hint:* First, clear Select All.)

7 Show all resources.

8 Without permanently renumbering them, sort the resources first by Group and then by Name. (*Hint:* Clear "Permanently renumber resources.")

9 Save and close the project file.

Review questions

1 Arranging tasks or resources in a specified sequence is called _____.

   A Filtering

   B Grouping

   C Sorting

   D Prioritizing

2 By _____, you can organize tasks and resources without changing the actual structure of a project.

   A Sorting

   B Grouping

   C Filtering

   D Prioritizing

3 By _____, you can show only those tasks or resources that meet your specified criteria, and hide all other information.

   A Filtering

   B Prioritizing

   C Sorting

   D Grouping

4 True or false? The grouping options that are available depend on the view you're working in.

5 True or false? You can apply an AutoFilter to an already filtered task or resource list.

6 After sorting a task or resource list several times, how do you return it to its original order?

Unit 7
Finalizing the task plan

Unit time: 45 minutes

Complete this unit, and you'll know how to:

A Display the critical path and slack, and edit effort-driven schedules to fine-tune a project.

B Resolve resource conflicts by using automatic and manual resource leveling.

Topic A: Finalizing schedules

Explanation
To manage a project effectively, you'll need to review your tasks to ensure that they meet the project objectives. You'll need to review the schedule and modify it as needed early in the planning process so that the project runs smoothly in the implementation phase. After making revisions, you can adjust the schedule to meet the project deadline.

The critical path

When you analyze a project schedule, you need to be aware of the project's critical tasks. *Critical tasks* are those tasks that must be completed on time for the project to finish on schedule. Changes made in critical tasks directly affect the finish date of the project. For example, if you increase the duration of a critical task, the project completion date will be delayed. If you reduce the time it takes to complete a critical task, the project completion date will move up. The *critical path* is the sequence of all critical tasks in a project.

It's important to note that in terms of work performed, critical tasks might be no more or less important than any other project tasks. They are considered critical only because their duration directly affects the project's completion date.

Viewing critical tasks

To show critical tasks in Gantt Chart view, click the Format tab and check Critical Tasks. By default, Project displays critical tasks as red task bars. You can also switch to Detail Gantt view, which automatically displays critical tasks as red task bars.

Slack

Slack is the amount of time you can delay tasks without affecting the project schedule. More specifically, *free slack* is the amount of time a task can be delayed before it delays another task, and *total slack* is the amount of time a task can slip without delaying the project completion date.

Viewing slack in a schedule

To show available slack in Gantt Chart view, click the Format tab and check Slack. In the Chart pane, slack is indicated by thin bars extending to the right of task bars. You can also switch to Detail Gantt view, which automatically displays slack in your project.

Detail Gantt view also includes the Free Slack and Total Slack columns in the Sheet pane. You can always manually add those columns to a task list.

Do it!

A-1: Displaying critical tasks and free slack

The files for this activity are in Student Data folder **Unit 7\Topic A**.

Here's how	Here's why
1 Open Construction project	
Save the file as **My Construction project**	
2 Click the **Format** tab	
3 Check **Critical Tasks**	To show the critical tasks—tasks that will delay the project finish date if they don't finish on schedule.
Observe the critical tasks	By default, Project displays critical tasks as red task bars, while non-critical tasks remain blue. In this project, most tasks are critical.
4 In the Timeline, scroll to the end of the project	(From the blue bar, drag the Timeline to the right, past Finish.) You'll locate tasks that are not on the critical path.
Scroll down to view tasks 32 and 34	
5 Why are tasks 32 and 34 not on the critical path?	
6 Check **Slack**	(On the Format tab.) To show the available slack.
Observe the task bars for tasks 32 and 34	
	A black line extending from the task bars indicates the amount of slack a task has built in.
Point to the left edge of the slack line for task 34	A ScreenTip appears, indicating that this task has free slack up to 5/17.
Clear **Slack**	To turn off the slack lines.
7 In the Timeline, observe the project finish date	The project is set to finish on 6/26.

8 Observe task 35	This task, "Insulation," is on the critical path. It must be completed on time, or the project finish date will be delayed.
9 Change the duration of task 35 to **3** days	
Observe the project finish date	The project finish date was pushed out one day, to 6/27.
10 Click [↶]	(On the Quick Access toolbar.) To undo the last action.
Observe the project finish date	The project completion date returned to 6/26.
11 What would happen to the project finish date if you increased the duration of task 34 to five days?	
12 What would happen to the project finish date if you were to increase the duration of task 34 to 10 days?	
13 Clear **Critical Tasks**	On the Format tab.
14 Switch to Detail Gantt view	
Observe the Format tab	In Detail Gantt view, critical tasks and slack are displayed by default.
15 Scroll up to view tasks 32 and 34	
	Detail Gantt view shows the amount of free slack next to a task.
Drag the Sheet pane's border to the right to see both Slack columns	Detail Gantt view includes columns for both Free Slack and Total Slack.
16 Save your changes	

Effort-driven schedules

Explanation

Project uses the following scheduling formula:

```
Duration = Work (Effort) / Resource Units
```

When you add resources to or remove resources from an effort-driven task, the duration of the task is modified to reflect the impact of more or fewer resources, but the work needed to complete the task remains unchanged. This method is called *effort-driven scheduling*, and it's Project's default scheduling mode.

Consider a task in which the duration of work is four days, and two resources are assigned to it for eight hours per day. *Total effort* is calculated by multiplying the duration by the number of resources. The total effort on this task is 64 hours (8 hours multiplied by 4 days multiplied by 2 resources). If you add two more resources to this task, Project will decrease the task duration to two days, keeping the total effort constant.

Non-effort-driven tasks

If a task is not effort-driven, then either the duration or the resource units must remain constant. Disabling effort-driven scheduling for a fixed-duration task can help you determine the effect that adding or removing a resource will have on the total amount of work involved in a task.

To make a task non-effort-driven:

1 Double-click the task name to open the Task Information dialog box.
2 Click the Advanced tab.
3 Clear Effort driven and click OK.

Smart Tags

Sometimes when you change tasks, Project will display a Smart Tag to verify your changes or to resolve a conflict that might arise. Click the Smart Tag to display options, and select the one that fits the intent of your modification. A small green triangle in the upper-left corner of a cell in the Task Name field indicates a Smart Tag pertaining to that cell.

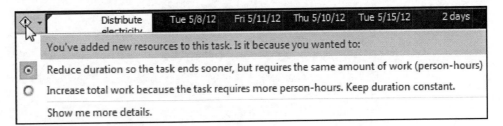

Exhibit 7-1: An example of Smart Tag options

Do it!

A-2: Editing effort-driven and non-effort-driven tasks

Here's how	Here's why
1 Observe the task bars for tasks 32 and 33	Task 32 ("Distribute heating, cooling") is blue, indicating that it's not a critical task. Task 33 ("Distribute electricity, phone, cabling") is red, indicating that it's a critical task.
2 Point to the task bar for task 33	The ScreenTip shows that this task has a scheduled duration of eight days.
In the Timeline, observe the project finish date	The project is scheduled to finish on June 26. The project is taking longer than desired, so you'll shorten the critical path to shorten the overall project.
3 Double-click **Distribute electricity, phone, cabling**	(Task 33.) To open the Task Information dialog box. You'll assign a new resource but will keep the Effort driven setting.
Click the **Advanced** tab	
Verify that **Effort driven** is checked	You'll observe the changes that Project makes in the task duration when Effort driven is checked.
4 Click the **Resources** tab	Notice that David, Jerry, Ann, and Susan are assigned to this task. You'll add another resource to decrease the task duration.
Click the row under Susan Gianni	A drop-down arrow appears in the cell.
Click the arrow and select **Contract laborers**	
5 In the Units field, enter **400**	To assign four contract laborers to this task at 100% effort each.
Click **OK**	With the added resources, Project automatically reduces the duration for this task from eight days to four days.
Deselect row 33	A Smart Tag is displayed on task 33.
6 Point to the green triangle and click as shown	To display the Smart Tag options.
Read the options	Project wants to verify the intent of the change in this task. In this case, the default selection is correct—you want to reduce the duration of the task.
7 Click the first option	To close it. The green triangle disappears.

8	Observe the task bars for tasks 32 and 33	Task 33 has changed from red to blue, indicating that it's no longer a critical task. Task 32 has changed from blue to red because it's now a critical task; any delay in completing task 32 will delay the project finish date.
	Observe the change in free slack	Now, task 33 and 34 have two days and three days of free slack, respectively.
	In the Timeline, observe the project finish date	The project finish date has been moved up four days, to June 22.
9	Switch to Gantt Chart view	
	On the Format tab, check **Critical tasks**	If necessary.
10	Observe the Duration field for task 11	(Scroll up.) This task has a duration of four days.
11	Double-click **Review blueprints**	You'll assign a third resource to this task.
	Click the **Advanced** tab	This task is currently effort-driven.
	Clear **Effort driven**	To keep the duration of the task constant regardless of how many resources are assigned to the task.
12	Click the **Resources** tab	An architect and Kathy Sinclair are currently assigned to this task.
	Click under Kathy Sinclair	
	From the Resources list, select **Pat Leary**, and click **OK**	To add a third resource to this task.
13	Observe the task duration	Project retains the original duration (four days) because it's not an effort-driven task.
14	Save and close the project file	

Topic B: Handling resource conflicts

Explanation

If a single resource is assigned to different tasks, that resource might exceed his or her work hours. Resources are *over-allocated* when they are scheduled to do more work than can be accomplished in the specified time.

Identifying resource over-allocation

In a resource view, it's easy to identify resources that are over-allocated—their information appears in bold red text, and the Indicators field displays a yellow warning icon. In Gantt Chart view, a task with an over-allocated resource assigned to it shows a red figure icon in the Indicators field.

Project also provides views that display the nature of resource allocation in your project. For example, Resource Sheet view displays several columns of information relevant to over-allocation, including Max Units and Cost/Use. Resource Graph view shows a graphical representation of the workload of a single resource. Resource Usage view shows a resource's total work and details of where the work is distributed on a calendar, as shown in Exhibit 7-2.

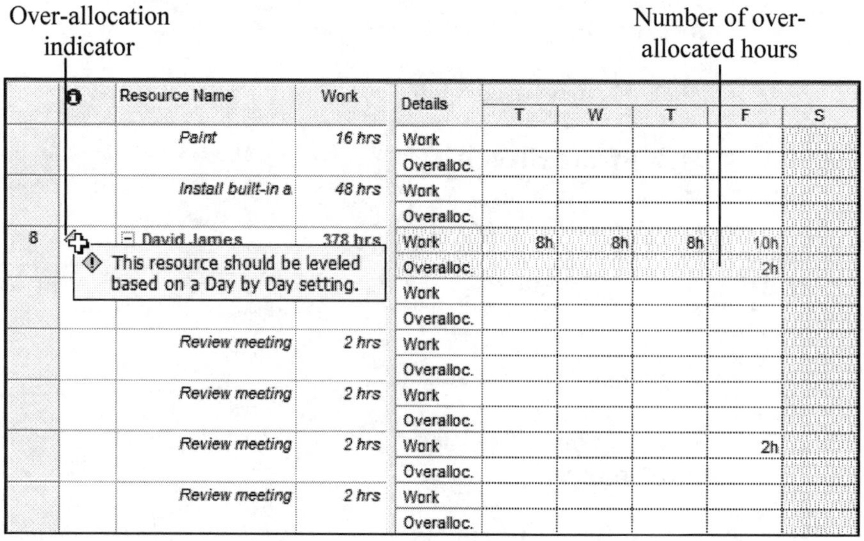

Exhibit 7-2: Resource Usage view, showing an over-allocated resource

Do it!

B-1: Viewing resource over-allocation

The files for this activity are in Student Data folder **Unit 7\Topic B**.

Here's how	Here's why
1 Open New office	From the current topic folder.
Save the file as **My New office**	
2 Scroll down to observe tasks 24–33	Several of these tasks involve over-allocated resources, indicated by the red figure in the Indicators field.
3 Switch to Resource Sheet view	Four resources are over-allocated, as indicated by the bold red text and yellow warning icons.
Point to a yellow icon	A ScreenTip appears, stating that this resource is over-allocated and should be leveled.
4 Switch to Resource Usage view	
Scroll down to locate an over-allocated resource	In Resource Usage view, you can quickly see all tasks assigned to a resource.
5 Observe the Details column	It provides a Work row to show how many hours of work a resource is assigned on individual days.
On the Format tab, check **Overallocation**	Now the Details column has rows for Work and Overallocation, so you can see the number of hours by which a resource is over-allocated.
Check **Remaining Availability**	By adding this row, you can quickly see areas on the calendar that represent unallocated time for a resource.
6 Press CTRL + G	To open the Go To dialog box.
Type **8** and click **OK**	To navigate directly to David James, whose resource ID is 8.
7 Scroll the Timeline so that the focus is on May	You can see that on Friday, May 4th, David is assigned to work 10 hours, two of which are over-allocated time. The following week, he is over-allocated by eight hours on four straight days.
8 Right-click **May 6, '12** and choose **Timescale...**	(At the top of the sheet.) You'll change the timescale to more easily identify days of the week.
From the Units list, select **Days** and click **OK**	
9 Save your changes	

Resolving resource over-allocation

Explanation

When you identify a resource that is over-allocated, you should act to resolve the over-allocation. How you resolve resource over-allocation will depend on the limitations of the project. Limitations might include the project budget, resource availability, and flexibility within the tasks that make up the schedule.

Resource leveling is the process of resolving resource over-allocation by adjusting resource assignments. You can level resources manually or let Project do it automatically. When you use Project's automatic leveling, tasks are delayed or split, which might not be the desired solution—especially because this can delay the project finish date. Also, if you want to reduce the workload of an over-allocated resource by assigning some of his or her tasks to an under-allocated resource, you can't use automatic leveling because it does not change who is assigned to tasks.

You can level resources manually in any of the following ways:

- Replace the over-allocated resource with an under-allocated resource.
- Assign an additional resource to the task.
- Reduce the work assignments of a task and increase the duration for its completion.
- Increase the working time of the resource.

Do it!

B-2: Discussing resource over-allocation

Questions and answers
1 If a resource is assigned to more than one task in the same time period, how would you resolve the over-allocation?
2 If a group of four contract laborers is allocated at 500%, how would you resolve this over-allocation?
3 If a part-time resource is assigned full-time to a task, how might you resolve this resource over-allocation?
4 Why is it important to use Project's automatic leveling feature carefully?

Filtering resources

Explanation

When you need to resolve resource issues such as over-allocation, it can be helpful to narrow down your resource list by filtering for a particular group, cost, or some other category. For example, if you want to use Resource Usage view to look for resources that might be available to fill in for an over-allocated resource, you can use the Filter list on the View tab to focus on only those resources that meet a certain criterion.

Do it!

B-3:   Filtering for specific resources

Here's how	Here's why
1 Click the **View** tab	You'll look for resources in the Labor group that can reduce David James's workload for the week of May 7.
2 From the Filter list, select **Group...**	To open the Group dialog box.
Type **labor** and click **OK**	To show only resources in the Labor group.
3 Look for resources that might be available the week of May 7	(Scroll down the list.) All resources in this group are already busy during most of the days that David is over-allocated. Laurie Macurthy and Tim Walson have some time available on Friday, but it won't be enough to resolve David's over-allocation.
4 Save your changes	

Leveling resources

Explanation

You can use the Level Resource command on the Resource tab to automatically level an over-allocated resource. When you use this command, Project applies the settings in the Leveling Options dialog box. To open this dialog box and change the leveling options, click Leveling Options on the Resource tab.

As mentioned earlier, when you use automatic resource leveling (using the Level Resources command), you might not always like the results. For example, Project might delay or split a task, and this could affect the project finish date.

Manual resource leveling

By manually leveling a resource, you have more control over how you resolve resource over-allocation. For example, if a resource is allocated to work on two tasks that are scheduled at the same time, you can manually change the units so that the resource works on both tasks at 50%.

To level a resource manually, double-click the task name that has an over-allocation. In the Task Information dialog box, click the Resources tab and edit the resource assignment as needed.

Do it! **B-4: Leveling a resource**

Here's how	Here's why
1 Observe the over-allocated hours for the week of May 7	(Scroll up, if necessary.) David is over-allocated from Tuesday through Friday.
2 Locate the tasks that David is assigned to this week	(Scroll down past the Review meetings.) Starting that Tuesday, David is assigned full time to both "Distribute heating, cooling" and "Distribute electricity, phone, cabling."
3 Click the **Resource** tab	
Point to **Level Resource**	To read the ScreenTip for this command. This command is based on the settings in the Leveling Options dialog box.
4 Click **Leveling Options**	To open the Leveling Options dialog box. Project will look for over-allocations on a day-by-day basis, and the date range spans the entire project.
Click **OK**	
5 Click **Level Resource**	To open the Level Resources dialog box.
Verify that **David James** is selected in the list	
Click **Level Now**	David James is no longer over-allocated.
6 Observe the changes in his task assignments	On Tuesday, David's work has been split between "Frame internal walls" and "Distribute heating, cooling." Also, he has been taken off the task "Distribute electricity, phone, and cabling." This may or may not be the desired solution.
7 Switch to Gantt chart view	
Scroll down to the project completion milestone	The automatic resource leveling has pushed back the project completion date from 6/22 to 6/29.
8 Click [↰]	To return to Resource Usage view.
Click **Cancel**	If you're prompted to choose a group.
Click [↰] again	To undo the resource leveling.

9	Select **Distribute heating, cooling**	In the Resource Usage sheet.
	Switch to Gantt chart view	
10	Double-click **Distribute heating, cooling**	To open the Task Information dialog box.
	Click the **Resources** tab	
11	In the Resource Name list, select **David James**	You'll replace this resource.
	From the Resource Name list, select **Contract laborers**	Contract laborers will now be assigned at 100% to this task.
	Click **OK**	To replace David James with a contract laborer. David James is no longer over-allocated from 5/7 through 5/10 because he is no longer over-allocated for this task.
12	Switch to Resource Usage view	
	Open the Go To dialog box	
	Navigate to David James, starting in the week of 5/7/12	Enter 8 in the ID field, enter 5/7/12 in the Date field, and click OK.
13	Verify that David James is no longer over-allocated this week	David is no longer assigned to the task "Distribute heating, cooling." His name is still red because he remains over-allocated on other tasks.
14	Switch to Gantt chart view	
	Navigate to the project completion milestone	This manual resource leveling solution did not affect the project finish date.
15	Save and close the project file	

Unit summary: Finalizing the task plan

Topic A   In this topic, you learned about **critical tasks**, **slack**, and how to view them. You used **Detail Gantt view** to observe the critical path and tasks with slack, and you learned about the difference between **effort-driven tasks** and **non-effort-driven tasks**. You learned how changing a task's effort type can affect the project schedule.

Topic B   In this topic, you learned how to identify resource **over-allocation** and use Resource Usage view to observe assigned work and over-allocated work. You learned important considerations pertaining to **resource leveling**, and you learned how to level resources automatically, using the Level Resource command, and manually, for more control over how an over-allocation is resolved.

Independent practice activity

In this activity, you'll assign a resource to a task without changing the duration. Then, you'll assign a resource to a task to change the task duration. You'll also view resource over-allocations and level an over-allocated resource.

The files for this activity are in Student Data folder **Unit 7\Unit summary**.

1 Open New office building.

2 Save the file as **My New office building**.

3 Assign Jerry Davis to the task "Excavate for foundation" without changing the duration of the task. (*Hint:* Clear Effort driven, if necessary.)

4 Assign Curt Allen to the task "Install drainage" to reduce the task duration.

5 Switch to Resource Allocation view.

6 In the Resource Usage pane, scroll down and select Ann Salinski to view her tasks in the Leveling Gantt pane.

7 Level Ann Salinski by replacing her with Joe Simmons for the task "Distribute heating, cooling." (*Hint:* In the Leveling Gantt pane, double-click "Distribute heating, cooling" and change the resource.)

8 Save and close the project file.

9 Close Microsoft Project.

Review questions

1 What are two ways you can view the critical path?

2 Which of the following is Project's scheduling formula?

A Duration = Work (Effort) / Resource Units

B Work = Resource Units / Duration

C Duration = Resource Units / Max Units

D Work = Max Units / Duration

3 What's the difference between free slack and total slack?

4 How are over-allocated resources displayed in resource views?

5 What are two ways that you can manually level an over-allocated resource?

6 True or false? The action that Project takes when you use the Level Resource command is determined by the settings in the Leveling Options dialog box.

Course summary

This summary contains information to help you bring the course to a successful conclusion. Using this information, you will be able to:

A Use the summary text to reinforce what you've learned in class.

B Determine the next courses in this series (if any), as well as any other resources that might help you continue to learn about Microsoft Project 2010.

Topic A: Course summary

Use the following summary text to reinforce what you've learned in class.

Unit summaries

Unit 1

In this unit, you learned about basic **project management concepts** and about the various project views. You identified **interface components** and the elements of a **Gantt chart**. You also learned how to create projects and how to set the **start date** for a project. You then learned how to use the Project Help window.

Unit 2

In this unit, you learned how to **create a task list** in both manual and automatic scheduling mode. You learned how to set **task durations** and change the default scheduling mode for all new files. You also learned how to modify a task list by adding, deleting, and rearranging tasks. You then learned how to format information in the Sheet pane, establish a project's **Work Breakdown Structure**, insert a project summary task, and create **summary tasks** and **subtasks**. Finally, you learned how to hide and show subtasks, hide columns in the Sheet pane, insert **milestones**, and apply **Gantt Chart styles**.

Unit 3

In this unit, you learned how to establish a **schedule** by linking and unlinking tasks. You learned about **task dependencies**, and you learned how to change task predecessors and set **lag time** and **lead time** to fine-tune a schedule. You also learned how to insert recurring tasks, work in Network Diagram view, and modify **task relationships**. You then learned how to use the Timeline to navigate a Gantt chart and how to apply **task types** and **task constraints**.

Unit 4

In this unit, you learned how to create a **base calendar** and change the working time. You also learned how to create a resource pool and a **resource calendar**, assign resources to tasks, and create and apply a **task calendar**. You then learned how to record project costs and use the **Cost table** in Gantt Chart view.

Unit 5

In this unit, you learned how to work in **Calendar view** and **Resource Form view**. You learned that form views provide detailed information about an individual task or resource. You also learned how to add tasks to the **Timeline**, format the Timeline, and share the Timeline with stakeholders via other Office 2010 applications, such as Outlook and PowerPoint. You learned how to work with and create **tables**. Finally, you learned how to **display WBS outline numbers** in a separate column and directly in the Task Name column.

Unit 6

In this unit, you learned how to apply **filters** to focus on a specific set of tasks or resources and hide information you don't need to see. You learned how to highlight information, apply AutoFilters, and create custom filters. You also learned how to **group tasks** and resources to organize project information. Finally, you learned how to **sort** tasks and resources.

Unit 7

In this unit, you learned about **critical tasks** and **slack**, and how to view them. You also learned about the difference between **effort-driven tasks** and non-effort-driven tasks. You then learned how to identify **resource over-allocation** and use Resource Usage view to observe assigned work and over-allocated work. Finally, you learned how to **level resources** automatically and manually to resolve resource conflicts.

Topic B: Continued learning after class

It is impossible to learn how to use any software effectively in a single day. To get the most out of this class, you should begin working with Microsoft Project to perform real tasks as soon as possible. We also offer resources for continued learning.

Next courses in this series

This is the first course in this series. The next course in this series is:

- *Microsoft Project 2010: Advanced*
  - Work with templates and data from Office programs
  - Track progress against a baseline
  - Analyze and update a project
  - Create and customize reports
  - Customize the Project environment
  - Manage multiple projects
  - Exchange project information with stakeholders

Other resources

For more information, visit www.axzopress.com.

Glossary

Base calendar

The calendar that defines the working days and working hours for a project. The Standard calendar is the default base calendar.

Calendar view

A view that displays your project dates chronologically and displays, in calendar format, tasks scheduled for a specific day, week, or month.

Constraints

The limitations imposed on a project.

Critical path

The series of tasks that must be completed on schedule for a project to finish on time.

Critical task

A task on the critical path. If a critical task is delayed, it affects the project schedule.

Dependencies

Attributes that define the way in which tasks are related or linked.

Duration

The time from start to finish that it takes to complete a task.

Filters

Tools used to view only those tasks or resources that meet specified criteria.

Finish-to-Start task dependency

A relationship in which the start of a task depends on the completion of its predecessor task.

Fixed cost

A cost that remains the same despite resources being added or taken away.

Fixed Duration task

A task that has a constant time value; even if you increase the resources allocated to the task, the duration remains the same.

Fixed Unit task

A task that has a constant quantity or units-of-resource value.

Fixed Work task

A task in which the total work to be performed has a constant value. The total amount of work performed on a task is the sum of resources used on that task.

Gantt bar

See *Task bar*.

Gantt Chart view

Project 2010's default view (with the Timeline). It consists of the Sheet pane and the Chart pane.

Lag time

A delay that adds extra time after the completion of a task.

Lead time

The overlap between dependent tasks.

Material resource

An item that is used to perform work on a task; for example paint, wood, steel, or fuel.

Milestone

An item that represents the completion of a major project phase or activity.

Network Diagram view

A view that displays your project as a flowchart.

Nodes

Boxes that represent tasks in Network Diagram view.

Overtime cost

A variable cost that is incurred to pay a resource for the hours it has worked during the overtime working hours as defined in a project.

Per-use cost

A variable cost that is incurred for the use of every unit of a resource in a task. Per-use cost is commonly used for resource materials, such as gravel, wood, and paint.

Predecessor task

A task that must start or finish before another task can begin.

Project

A one-time, organized effort that leads toward meeting a specific goal and that has a definite start and end.

Project life cycle

The four phases of a project: the initial phase, the planning phase, the implementation phase, and the close-out phase.

Project management

The application of knowledge, skills, tools, and techniques to accomplish activities or tasks to meet the objectives set for a project.

Project manager

The person who has the primary role of directing the project's flow and the communication between its participants.

Project summary task

The highest level of your task list. Use the project summary task to display the objective of your project.

Recurring task

A task that occurs at regular intervals during a project.

Resource calendar

A calendar that contains information that is specific to a resource. For example, a resource calendar might show a resource's vacation schedule.

Resource Form view

A view that provides detailed information on a single resource.

Resource Graph view

A view used to identify the allocation of work or the cost of resources over a specific time frame.

Resource leveling

The process of resolving resource over-allocation by adjusting resource assignments for a project.

Resource over-allocation

A state in which resources are scheduled to do more work than can be accomplished in the specified time.

Resource pool

The list of resources available for assignment on a project.

Resource Sheet view

A view used to enter resource information.

Resource Usage view

A view used to estimate resource utilization.

Risk management

The preparation for uncertainties that might occur during a project.

Scheduling

The timing and sequencing of tasks.

Scope creep

A gradual addition of work that eventually makes original cost and schedule estimates unachievable.

Sorting

The act of organizing tasks and resources in a specified sequence.

Stakeholders

The people and organizations that have a vested interest, or stake, in the project. Stakeholders include the project manager, decision makers, customers, vendors, and employees who will contribute to the project.

Standard cost

A variable cost that is incurred to pay a resource for the hours it has worked on a task during the standard working hours as defined in a project.

Start-to-Start dependency

A relationship in which two tasks can be done concurrently.

Subtasks

Tasks that are indented below a summary task.

Task

Each activity in a project.

Task bar

A horizontal bar in the Chart pane that indicates the time allocated for a task. Task bars are also called *Gantt bars*.

Task list

The tasks that must be accomplished to complete the project.

Total effort

A value calculated by multiplying the duration by the number of resources.

Variable cost

A cost that changes with the frequency and amount of time a resource is used.

Variance

The difference between the actual and planned costs.

Work Breakdown Structure (WBS)

The hierarchical structure of a project's task list. The project summary task is the highest level of the WBS, and the other tasks are broken down to their lowest manageable levels.

Work resources

The people and equipment that perform work on a task.

Index

A

AutoFilters, 6-4

B

Backstage view, 1-10
Base calendars, creating and applying, 4-2

C

Calendar view, 1-7, 5-2
Close-out phase, 1-3
Constraints, types of, 1-2, 3-17
Cost resources, 4-6
Cost table, 4-19
Costs, types of, 4-17
Critical path, 3-13, 7-2

D

Days, working vs. nonworking, 4-2
Duration, entering, 2-5

E

Effort-driven scheduling, 7-5

F

Filters
    Applying, 6-2, 7-11
    Creating, 6-6
Fixed costs, 4-17
Fixed Duration tasks, 3-16
Fixed Unit tasks, 3-16
Fixed Work tasks, 3-16
Form views, 5-4
Free slack, 7-2

G

Galleries, 1-10
Gantt Chart styles, applying, 2-19
Gantt Chart view, 1-6, 1-12
Groups
    Applying to tasks or resources, 6-8
    Creating, 6-10

H

Help window, 1-19

I

Implementation phase, 1-3
Initial phase, 1-3

L

Lag time, 3-6
Lead time, 3-6

M

Material resources, 4-6
Milestones, 1-2
    Inserting, 2-18
Monitoring phase, 1-3

N

Network Diagram view, 1-6, 3-10
Nonworking days, 4-2

O

Outline levels for tasks, 2-15
Over-allocation, 7-8
    Resolving, 7-10
Overtime cost, 4-17

P

Per-use cost, 4-17
Planning phase, 1-3
Predecessor tasks, 3-2, 3-5
Project management
    Defined, 1-2
    Typical tasks in, 1-5
Projects
    Constraints, 1-2
    Defining properties of, 1-16
    Phases of, 1-2

Q

Quick Access toolbar, 1-9

R

Recurring tasks, 3-8
Resource calendars, creating, 4-8
Resource graphs, 4-10
Resource leveling, 7-10, 7-12
Resource list, sorting, 6-13

Resource pools, 4-6
Resource Sheet view, 1-7, 4-6
Resource Usage view, 1-7
Resources
    Assigning, 4-10, 4-12
    Defined, 1-5
    Over-allocated, 7-8
    Types of, 4-6
Ribbon, 1-9
Risk management, 1-4

S

Scheduling
    Automatic, 2-5
    Effort driven, 7-5
    Manual vs. automatic, 2-2
    Setting mode for new files, 2-8
Scope creep, 1-4
Sheet pane
    Adding WBS column to, 5-10
    Formatting, 2-12
    Hiding columns in, 2-16
Slack, 7-2
Smart Tags, 7-5
Sorting tasks or resources, 6-12
Split views, 5-4
Stakeholders, 1-4
Standard cost, 4-17
Subtasks, 2-13
    Hiding and showing, 2-15
Successor tasks, 3-2
Summary tasks, 2-13

T

Tables
    Adding WBS column to, 5-10
    Creating, 5-10
Task calendars, 4-14

Task dependencies, 3-2
    Types of, 3-12
Task list, 2-2
    Rearranging tasks in, 2-11
    Sorting, 6-12
Tasks
    Adding, 2-9
    Applying lag or lead time to, 3-7
    Converting to milestones, 2-18
    Critical, 3-13, 7-2
    Deleting, 2-9
    Linking, 3-2
    Moving up or down in the WBS, 2-15
    Non-effort-driven, 7-5
    Recurring, 3-8
    Specifying duration of, 2-5
    Types of, 3-16
    Unlinking, 3-2
Timeline, 1-5, 1-9, 3-13
    Copying into other applications, 5-8
    Formatting, 5-6
Total effort, calculating, 7-5
Total slack, 7-2

U

User-controlled scheduling, 2-2

V

Variable costs, 4-17
Views, 1-5
    Filtering, 6-2
    Splitting, 5-4

W

Work Breakdown Structure (WBS), 1-6, 2-13, 5-10
Work resources, 4-6